do less

A minimalist guide to a simplified, organized, and happy life

Rachel Jonat

Avon, Massachusetts

Published by

Adams Media, a division of F+W Media, Inc.

57 Littlefield Street, Avon, MA 02322. U.S.A.

www.adamsmedia.com

ISBN 10: 1-4405-7363-8
ISBN 13: 978-1-4405-7363-7
eISBN 10: 1-4405-7364-6
eISBN 13: 978-1-4405-7364-4

Printed in the United States of America.

10 9 8 7 6 5 4 3 2

Library of Congress Cataloging-in-Publication Data

Jonat, Rachel.
Do less / Rachel Jonat.
pages cm
ISBN-13: 978-1-4405-7363-7 (pb)
ISBN-10: 1-4405-7363-8 (pb)
ISBN-13: 978-1-4405-7364-4 (ebook)
ISBN-10: 1-4405-7364-6 (ebook)
1. Simplicity. I. Title.
BJ1496.J66 2014
646.7--dc23

2013047398

This book is available at quantity discounts for bulk purchases.
For information, please call 1-800-289-0963.

Contents

Introduction 5

What Is Minimalism? 7

Home 25

Work 71

Money 99

Life 133

Your Minimalist Life 173

Introduction

Tired, broke, and stressed out? Overwhelmed with cluttered junk drawers, a bursting calendar, and mile-long to-do lists? Feel like you're always behind on bills and work? The answer to the ailments of modern living and the constant busy-ness we all experience isn't a new organizational system, an app, or a manifesto on how to do it all.

It's minimalism.

Minimalism can help you get rid of the clutter in your home, life, and work so you can spend your time, money, and energy on the things you really love. The essence of minimalism, originally a movement in design and art, is using the fewest elements to create the maximum effect.

Voluntary simplicity is the act of embracing minimalism. Note the word "voluntary." Yes, you have a choice. Do you want to live with clutter, with things you don't need or use? Do you want to spend your hard-earned money on clothes you never wear and décor you have to spend your free time dusting? Or do you want to live in a soothing, spacious home that's easy to clean and have all the time and resources you need for the activities and people you enjoy? If you scale back your possessions and commitments to just what you really need, you will have more time and energy for those things that truly bring you joy and enrich your life.

Minimalism can make your living room more inviting, bring you more sleep, and help you find your dream job. But where do you start? If you're already tired, stressed out, and broke, how do you find the time to declutter your home, the energy to resist the sale signs, and the resources to create that streamlined life you dream about? This book will show you how.

This is a simple, realistic guide to getting simple. You won't have to spend weeks or years emptying your garage. You don't have to give up your favorite television shows. You don't have to live like a monk, eating meals out of your one pot while leaning over the sink because you sold your dining room table. You won't find cutthroat checklists or complicated philosophical exercises. Just simple, easy ways to quickly declutter your life and home so you can focus on what you love most.

What Is Minimalism?

> **Life is not complex. We are complex. Life is simple, and the simple thing is the right thing.**

—Oscar Wilde

As a lifestyle, minimalism is using the simplest and fewest things to create the maximum effect possible. It's about removing whatever isn't contributing to the desired outcome. The minimalist lifestyle movement centers around living very simply and with very little.

Minimalism *Anyone* Can Embrace

Some proponents of minimalism count everything they own and live nomadically. They've found peace with very few possessions and living in small spaces. Although their resolve is admirable, it's also extreme and certainly not for everyone.

Instead, this book shows you how to adopt the essence of minimalism, the "do more with less" edict, to tailor your life to include just the things you truly need and enjoy. This book is about getting more of what you really want in your life. We'll examine a few more radical ideas for scenarios like getting out of debt or transitioning to a new career; however, the ideas in this book are mainly geared toward those of us looking for a bit more time and space—without having to move to Ecuador or give up every single small luxury in our lives. This is a practical guide to minimalism and how to make small changes that have a big impact.

> ## This book is about getting more of what you really want in your life.

After you take away the things, both physical and mental, gathering dust that you haven't used in years, if ever, you'll find that you suddenly have space to enjoy things you love, and the energy to achieve those secret goals you shelved away because you didn't think you had the time or money for them.

You might need time and space for a whole range of reasons: the fitness goals, the annual resolution to get more sleep, the household chores that pile up. You'll see how embracing minimalism will help you get those things done.

Minimalism is also a way to reimagine your life on a grander scale. It sounds dramatic, but it's true. Removing what is unnecessary in your life gives you the space and time to revisit old dreams and create new ones. If you've put away dreams because you thought they were unattainable, it's time to say hello to them again. Using minimalism to streamline a few areas of your life can help you finish writing your novel, run your first 5k, or even take a three-month sabbatical from your job to spend the summer in the south of France. No far-flung goal is too small or too big.

Why Do You Need Minimalism?

The busy-ness of twenty-first-century living has most of us mired in stuff and obligations we can't remember why we bought or signed up for in the first place. We struggle to make it through the workweek without at least one takeout meal, and we feel pinched in every avenue of our lives. We don't have enough time for breakfast, let alone time for all those tasks on our long and ever-growing to-do lists.

This abundance of things and activities is relatively new. In fact, life used to be very simple: Securing shelter and food were the goals. Cavemen and -women didn't suffer from paralysis by analysis, because they didn't have forty pairs of shoes and half a dozen social commitments every weekend. No hunter-gatherers lost sleep over plans for a bathroom renovation. As recently as a hundred years ago, most people only owned a few outfits and wore the same pair of shoes every day. Most families lived in homes that had just a few rooms and children shared a bedroom. An orange was considered an exotic food. Pinterest didn't exist. These were much simpler times with fewer choices for leisure-time activities and nondiscretionary income.

With many choices and opportunities comes great responsibility. We are living in an abundant yet complicated era. Work is no longer limited to the office, socializing is no longer limited by the need to meet face-to-face, and shopping is no longer limited to store hours. Today we can buy, socialize, and be entertained whenever we like. We have more demands on our attention and time than anyone a hundred years ago could have imagined.

It's these abundant choices and these constant demands that can undo your greatest intentions.

- You want a tidy closet with fashionable, easy-to-wear pieces, but after a hard day at the office, you shop away your stress at a sale and come home with outfits bought on impulse.

- You'd like more time for your favorite hobbies, but you seem to lose most of your daylight hours to work, commuting, and keeping your home organized and all your stuff in its place.

- You want to be in the moment and have meaningful conversations with your closest friends, but your cell phone keeps buzzing with text messages, e-mail notifications, and calls.

- When you try to stick to a budget, you end up just seeing more sale signs in store windows and your inbox.

How do you clear the endless clutter from your life and home when you see *more* and *new* and *bigger* and *better* at every corner?

Minimalism. Minimalism can help you tune out these distractions and focus on the simple pleasures in your life. You don't need a time machine to take you back to a simpler life; you can create that simple life today. You can enjoy the abundance available nowadays on your own terms, as you see fit. You can Do Less and enjoy more.

The Happiness Factor

Having so many choices allows us to clutter our daily lives with a lot of tasks, obligations, and sometimes even hobbies and friendships that don't actually make us happy. We're so busy checking things off a list we don't have time to wonder why they're on the list in the first place.

Think of the simple joys in your life, the ones that don't require opening your wallet or checking your e-mail. They could be things like getting up early to make a hot breakfast before work, calling your friend in another time zone for an evening chat, taking a walk after dinner, resting in your freshly vacuumed living room, sleeping in on a Saturday, or making bread from scratch.

If you have trouble thinking of things that make you happy, consider the last twenty-four or forty-eight hours. When did you feel your best? What were the highlights of those days? They could be small or big moments: a great conversation over a meal with friends, an extra-long shower, success on a work project, or finally painting the bathroom after putting it off for many weekends. If your best moment of the week was kicking your feet up and not having to do anything, that's okay too.

Next, make note of the big and small things that *didn't* make you happy or that cast a dark cloud over your day: the argument you had with your spouse, the complicated dinner you tried to pull off on a Wednesday night that caused you to eat an hour late and left your kitchen looking like a hurricane hit, or the shocking credit card bill that soured your mood for a day. Look at how or if these unhappy moments were tied to other negative things. Did the argument with your spouse come on the heels of opening that credit card bill that revealed a number of impulsive purchases?

When you think about what brings you happiness, note how little stuff is actually involved. A nice conversation over tea, a healthy meal, sleep, exercise—none of them requires deep closets full of stuff to enjoy. When you figure out what's making you happy, it's easy to let go of the things and obligations in your life that aren't making you happy. It's also easier to go through your possessions and clearly see what you use enough to justify keeping. That massive DVD collection doesn't seem so important once you realize you haven't watched a DVD in months and the rows of plastic cases require constant dusting and take up all the shelf space in your small living room. Just consider, what would your home and life look like without all that stuff?

> **When you think about what brings you happiness, note how little stuff is actually involved.**

Minimalism can bring more happiness into your life. Some of that happiness is derived from simple pleasures; other happiness will come from creating the time and motivation for the challenging tasks that bring with them long-term contentment and satisfaction. It may seem like a strange concept, but yes, that DVD collection can hold you back from career leaps, financial freedom, and even that extra twenty minutes a day to linger over a cup of coffee and the newspaper.

Decision Fatigue

Consider this common scenario: As your day begins, you probably have all the willpower you need to eat a healthy breakfast. Your morning starts out well at the office and you're answering critical e-mails succinctly and easily and plowing through your to-do list. Then you're faced with three different options for lunch: a last-minute invitation to a birthday celebration, take-out from a gourmet deli, or your healthy leftovers from home. Your mouth is salivating at the thought of the deli's famous Philly cheesesteak and you'd love to escape the office for a celebratory meal, but you reluctantly eat your bagged lunch.

In the afternoon your willpower and productivity wane. You indulge in a piece of birthday cake, even though you told yourself you wouldn't eat any. The afternoon stretches on and you find yourself struggling to focus. A small decision necessary to move a project forward seems incredibly hard to make and you spend much longer than you anticipated debating each choice. You finally make a choice and then quickly make a larger, more important and much more costly decision. On the way home from work, you hit the grocery store for a dozen items. You spend five minutes looking at all the canned tomato options and calculating which is the cheapest. After saving yourself eight cents on the tomatoes you don't have the time or the energy to do the same for laundry detergent, so you end up quickly grabbing something that is familiar and missing the sale sign that could have saved you $3. By this point, your legs are tired and you can't face the gym workout you'd planned to face. You're starving too, so you grab some take-out because it's too late to go home and cook now, even though you just went to the grocery store. The rest of your evening, one you planned to use for some small projects around the house, devolves into a night of zoning out in front of the television.

We make hundreds of small and big decisions every day. What to eat, what to wear, when to leave, and what brand of toothpaste to buy are all relatively small choices, but each one depletes your ability to make subsequent decisions. Every single choice, big or small, saps some of your energy for the next choice—which is why by late afternoon or early evening, you are ready to throw in the towel on any grand plan you had when the day started. You're ready to spend more money than you intended buying things you're not sure you need and to eat two slices of cake when you promised yourself you would have none.

Decision-making depletes your willpower. In the book *Willpower: Rediscovering the Greatest Human Strength,* authors Roy Baumeister and John Tierney describe researchers who tested the willpower of two different sets of college students by placing the students' hands in ice-cold water. One set of students kept their hands in the water for an average of twenty-eight seconds and the other set of students kept their hands in for an average of sixty-seven seconds. The students who held their hands in the freezing water longer had just spent time contemplating, not deciding on, sets of products, whereas the low-willpower group of students had just spent time choosing between products, deciding which ones they wanted more. The experiment confirms the willpower-depleting nature of making decisions.

This loss of willpower from making many decisions is called "decision fatigue" and it's one of the best reasons to streamline your life and home with minimalism. The minimalist life turns those small decisions into routines or eliminates them completely. The Do Less attitude allows you to save that precious willpower for doing the wonderful big and small things you want more of in your life. There are lots of easy, small ways to reduce decision fatigue, such as:

- Bring coffee from home every morning and use the energy usually reserved for resisting the croissants displayed at the café register for that challenging work project.

- Wear the same series of outfits Monday through Friday and never deliberate over what to wear to work again. Use that decision-making energy to get yourself out the door to an evening yoga class or to that book reading you've been meaning to attend.

- Research three options and then buy one. We often overwhelm ourselves with decision fatigue when we have to buy something. Instead of looking at every item on the shelf, examine three options and then choose one from that much smaller list. This works for buying anything from a pair of jeans to dishwasher detergent.

The scary and awesome side of decision fatigue is that it affects both decisions that are worth one dollar and those that are worth thousands of dollars. When you reduce the choices in your life with minimalism, you free up willpower for the things that have a big impact on your life.

Actually *Use* Your Beautiful Things

The Home section of this book is a practical guide for decluttering your physical space. You can expect a revealing and sometimes emotional journey as you follow the steps to rid clutter from each room of your home. First, you'll ask yourself, how did I get this much stuff? All of us are shocked when we truly realize how much we have. Second, why am I not using some of this stuff? One of the tenets of a minimalist life is to only have things that you use regularly. This doesn't mean you have to get rid of luxuries—instead, it means you'll now be sipping a spritzer from your wedding crystal on a boring Wednesday night and wearing your prized cashmere sweater weekly.

Beautiful things should be used and seen. If something is far too precious to be used for its intended purpose, what is the point of owning it? What is the point of storing it and caring for it if it's not useful? Embrace everyday luxury, and if an item breaks or is ruined, celebrate that you got more out of it than you would have if you kept it in a closet for years.

Clutter Is a Result of Forgetting Yourself

Have you ever looked through your closet or cabinets and wondered, why did I ever buy that? Often, clutter is the result of good intentions gone wrong. Perhaps you're a jeans and T-shirt person but decided, at the influence of a friend with drastically different taste than your own, to buy a few pieces of clothing in a style you aren't really comfortable wearing. The clothes end up languishing in your closet after you've worn them once. Or you buy some home gym equipment that's on sale, thinking that you'll start working out at home. The gym equipment gets little use because you actually like working out with a buddy or playing team sports. That set of barbells was for someone else's life, not yours. That's how you end up with closets, drawers, and garages filled with good—but misguided—intentions.

It's easy to stumble into clutter if you forget your own unique likes and loves. Instead of embracing and celebrating what you truly like, you get distracted by what you think you *should* like. Magazines, Pinterest, and our peers all inundate us with styles and DIY projects and the latest crafting craze. As you sift through all the pictures and blog posts and knitting patterns, you start to think that you're supposed to do and buy all this stuff. You accidentally brainwash yourself into hobbies you don't really like and clothes that don't suit your lifestyle or your body.

It's so easy to forget who you truly are when you are constantly watching and reading the highlights and glories of everyone else.

- Facebook status updates from a destination you don't even want to go to make you pine for more travel, even though you're a happy homebody.

- A friend with makeup skills and a love of lipstick makes you feel inferior with your natural touch-of-mascara look.

- Attending a precisely executed gourmet dinner party makes you run out and buy a cheeseboard and matching cheese knives, even though you mostly have people over for casual barbecues and the most exotic cheese in your house is marbled cheddar.

You forget who you are. You forget what's important to you, what makes you smile, what your talents and gifts are.

If you want to Do Less, you need to remove the ideas and dreams you took on because you thought they were the right things to *do*, instead of the right things for *you*. There really is enough time and space and energy in your day to do what you want to do. The trick is not to fill your time with things you *think* you should be doing. If something doesn't feed your soul or your family, it shouldn't get your money and it definitely shouldn't get your time. Minimalism will help you recapture yourself.

If You Can't Use It, Let Someone Else

You probably keep things for "someday" when you think you'll have time or the need to use them: the boxes of home décor in the attic, the skis that haven't been touched in six years, the silicone baking cups still in their package. You buy things hoping that they'll be a catalyst for change, dreaming that a shoe rack will keep your hallway clear or a pie tin will inspire you to bake more pies . . . but in the end, many of the things you buy to simplify your life end up cluttering it. Your good intentions linger in cupboards and attics and never get used. The good news?

Someone else can use all those things sitting around unused in your home.

As you change how you think about what you own and how much you really need, you can let go of unused things and let someone else use them. If you already have enough to keep your home running, to wear to work, to cook a meal with, to entertain yourself with, why do you need all those things that you aren't using? Lots of people out there will burn those candles, read those books, and wear those silk dresses. In fact, your clutter can:

- Be sold in thrift stores, where the proceeds help local charities.

- Help a family that has lost everything to rebuild.

- Earn cash at a garage sale or on eBay to help boost household income.

Your clutter can be used for good, and that's so much better than letting it gather dust.

Someday Is Not Today

One of the main reasons we keep things we don't use or need is we think someday we'll need them. Someday you'll mountain bike again. Someday you'll actually get that vintage dress repaired and tailored and wear it to a winter cocktail party.

Someday you'll wear those clothes that don't fit right now and someday you'll read that book and someday you'll finish that quilt you started in high school.

If you add up all the things in your home that you think you will use for a someday activity, you'll see that it would be impossible to use them all. You'll also see that if you packed your life with all these someday activities, you'd have no time or space for the things you love right now. Your home should contain only the things that you use today and now.

If you give something away that you need again "someday," you can buy it or borrow it. It's that simple. We'll talk more about strategies for sentimental clutter and ideas for simplifying each area of your home in the Home section.

Live Your Unlived Life

In the book *The War of Art: Break Through the Blocks and Win Your Inner Creative Battles,* screenwriter and fiction author Steven Pressfield names the inertia or futility we often feel when pursuing a goal. Pressfield calls our procrastination techniques "resistance" and describes all the ways we sabotage our own success. The author also talks about the two lives we live— the one we dream about, called the unlived life, and our actual lives. He says that living your unlived life comes from beating resistance.

The minimalist approach is another way to beat resistance and live your unlived life. As you peel back the layers of your stuff and your commitment to busy-ness, you'll find the space to live your unlived life. The distractions of stuff and clutter fall away and you're left with the essentials. From there, you find the time to climb those mountains you once thought unscalable. It doesn't matter if the "mountain" is simply getting to bed earlier or organizing your paperwork so tax time is a breeze. No goal is too small or too big. Whether you want to start your own business or simply want to stop tripping over all the shoes left near your front door, removing the resistance of clutter will allow you to realize those goals.

A Guide to Using This Book

This book offers hundreds of ideas for creating a decluttered, organized, and happy life with minimalism. Some of the ideas are radical and big, but most are small and simple. The best way to use this book is to implement the ideas that speak to your life and your goals.

- If you want to save money, look at the ideas for reducing your cost of living in the Money section. Once you've implemented them, move on to decluttering your home and selling things you aren't using.

- If you're stressed out with social obligations and feel short on time, use the ideas in the Life section to get more hours back in your day.

▦ If you feel overwhelmed every time you try to organize your home office, work through the Home section to pare down your things.

One of the best features of the minimalist approach is that you'll see benefits whether you use bits and pieces of it or make it the foundation of your entire life. Let's dive in—get ready to stress less and live more.

Home

> **Have nothing in your houses that you do not know to be useful, or believe to be beautiful.**
>
> —William Morris

You start with the best of intentions, thinking, *This kitchen appliance/vase/shoe rack will bring beauty to my home and make my life easier.* Yet, somehow the piece never solves your problem. It doesn't give you more time or space, and you end up dusting it for a decade while paying interest on it until you finally realize it just created more clutter.

Where You Are Now

Can you sit in your living room and read a book without seeing something that needs to be put away or cleaned or finished? Do you fall asleep looking at piles of laundry to sort and wash? Is your desk covered with bills to file or shred? Can you easily and quickly clean your home, or do you constantly have to stop to pick things up or move them before you can vacuum and wipe down counters?

It is no wonder we're stressed out when our homes are filled with unfinished craft projects, clutter we don't have space to store, and wardrobes that burst out of closets. Your home should be a haven. It should be a place to relax, rest, entertain, and work. It should be an expression of what you value— be that space to roll out a yoga mat, an inviting dining table for entertaining friends, or the perfect spot to display fresh-cut flowers.

How do you create this space, this home with room to breathe and play and sleep soundly, when you are overwhelmed with all the things that are stuffed inside it? In this chapter, you'll learn simple and quick ways to eliminate what's unnecessary from each room of your home and leave just what is purposeful and beautiful. You will learn how to make quick decisions on what stays and what goes so you can start living in a peaceful uncluttered home right now.

Before we tackle the seven spatulas jammed into your kitchen utensil drawer, let's talk about legacy. What would happen if you passed away and someone else, possibly a spouse or close relative, had to go through your home and empty it of your possessions? Would it be an easy task? Would you have thoughtfully kept things of value that could be passed on or sold or given away? Would your mementos and photos be carefully culled into a timeline of life events that your family could easily look through, enjoy, and quickly decide what parts of which they would like to keep for themselves? Or would the work of emptying your home be a great burden on someone you love?

These can be sobering and unpleasant thoughts, but if your first reaction is potential embarrassment, followed closely by motivation, then it's time to sort the ten boxes of high school memorabilia you've moved four times in seven years without opening once.

To quickly and easily declutter your home, think of it as an art gallery. It's time to curate your possessions into a simple expression of your purpose and your joys. There is no room for the unnecessary—those things you might need "someday," or things you keep solely because they were gifts. Let those go. Life is far too short to live with things you neither love nor need. Let's start with one of the most common problem areas—the kitchen.

Kitchen

Mark Bittman, author and *New York Times* columnist, claims even the best chefs can get by with a small set of kitchen tools. With his no-frills, $200–$300 collection of kitchen tools, Bittman is capable of cooking gourmet meals. Here is a no-frills kitchen supply list for people who cook gourmet meals at home:

- 8-inch chef's knife
- Instant-read thermometer
- 3 stainless steel nesting bowls
- Tongs
- 1 sheet pan
- Plastic cutting board
- Paring knife
- Can opener
- Vegetable peeler
- Colander
- 3 sizes of cast-aluminum saucepans
- Medium nonstick cast-aluminum pan
- Large, deep-sided heavy steel pan
- One lid
- Slotted spoon
- Skimmer
- Heat-resistant rubber spatula
- Bread knife
- Big whisk
- Food processor
- Salad spinner
- Microplane grater
- Coffee and spice grinder
- Immersion or stand blender
- Whetstone for knife sharpening

Most of us cook simple meals and rarely host formal dinner parties, yet have twice as many kitchen tools as Bittman suggests. Why do we have so much stuff in our kitchens? We confuse owning things with doing things. Owning a bread machine or bread loaf pans does not mean you will bake bread every week. As you weed through your cake pans and egg slicers, remember that the tools don't make the chef; the meal does.

What Do You Actually Cook?

The blueprint for going minimalist in the kitchen will be your six favorite meals that you cook regularly. You'll want to keep all the tools needed for them and your pantry stocked with whatever they require. Everything else can go. That includes the ice cream maker you used twice ten years ago, the canning supplies you had the best of intentions for but that are still in unopened boxes, and six of the seven paring knives in your utensil drawer. They can all go.

But what if you need those things someday? You just might. Perhaps in fifteen years, you'll have a formal dinner party and want to try your hand at making watermelon sorbet. Or your sister will bring you a box of peaches from her trip to the farmers' market and you'll suddenly be inspired to make jam. But you no longer have that ice cream maker, those canning supplies, and all those paring knives that would be so handy for peeling twenty pounds of peaches.

If the occasion arises where you might actually need items you've gotten rid of, here is what you do: You make do. You get resourceful. You ask friends if anyone can loan you an ice cream maker for a weekend. You learn how to make sorbet just using your freezer, a plastic bucket with a lid, and a timer reminding you to stir every four hours. You ask the last person who gave you homemade jelly as a gift if you can spend the afternoon at his house making jam in return for a few jars. There is already plenty of stuff in this world and the savvy minimalist both loans out her items when she can and borrows when needed.

> **If the occasion arises where you might actually need items you've gotten rid of, here is what you do: You make do.**

Dinnerware

Restaurants have it right: classic white plates are the perfect dinnerware. You can spend $100 on a meal or $10, but the food will be served on the same thing—a plain white dish. As you evaluate your dishes, be they fine china or everyday plates, consider streamlining to just what you use regularly, both in amount and type.

If you're going to keep fine china, use it. That might mean for take-out on a Friday night or for a leisurely Sunday brunch. Enjoy those beautiful dishes as often as you can. If the thought of anyone sawing up a steak on your fine dinner plates makes you nauseous, think about selling your china set. Anything "too good" to use has no purpose in a home.

Think carefully about how often you serve meals for more than six people. You may host Thanksgiving dinner every four years and need plates for twenty-four people, but it's not a weekly or even monthly occurrence. Unless you're hosting international dignitaries, it probably isn't a requirement that all the plates match or that the serving platters have a turkey motif on Thanksgiving. When, and if, you host a very large party, you can ask a friend to loan you dinnerware or even rent some for the occasion.

The extreme minimalist might only keep one bowl, plate, cup, and utensils per person in a household, requiring everyone to wash up after each meal. The moderate approach is to have enough dishware to fill your dishwasher. With the smallest bit of effort, you'll never be without a clean plate.

> ## Anything "too good" to use has no purpose in a home.

Pantry

Your pantry should be stocked with fresh, regularly used staples. Think beans, peanut butter, and canned tomatoes. Jars of capers and marinated artichokes, and other one-off ingredients that you don't use in your weekly meals often take up space in your pantry until you realize, usually a few years too late, that they are well past their sell-by date. Only purchase specialty items if you plan to use them up within a few weeks.

The other big reason for cluttered shelves of canned goods: not shopping with a list. Haphazard grocery shopping, forgetting what's actually in your cupboards, and getting lured in by sales or new products result in a stuffed pantry that's difficult to navigate and use. As you bring home new items, older food gets pushed to the back. When you finally get around to cleaning your cupboards, you find you have multiple opened boxes of crackers or cereal that are all stale because they got lost on your deep and packed shelves. Having fewer items in your pantry will reduce food waste, make grocery shopping easier, and speed up meal preparation.

In the Life section of this book, you'll read more about the importance of shopping with a list and meal planning. These are the cornerstones of using minimalism to simplify meal preparation and will greatly reduce the time you spend cooking and grocery shopping. An added bonus: you'll save money enjoying healthy meals at home instead of ordering take-out or eating fast food.

> **Having fewer items in your pantry will reduce food waste, make grocery shopping easier, and speed up meal preparation.**

Refrigerator

Here's a test: Can you clearly see the back of your refrigerator? Can you also quickly clean your refrigerator? If your refrigerator has long-expired sauces lining the door shelves and leftovers growing mold, it's time to go minimalist with your perishable food.

First, why do you have so much food in your home? Unless you live in the country without easy access to a grocery store, most homes only need a week's worth of fresh groceries and a month's worth of canned items. Anything more and you are likely to lose more money in food waste than you save by buying in bulk. Yes, some people are excellent at buying mass quantities of food, preparing it, and storing it. But most of us have deep freezers full of freezer-burned meat and don't even get halfway through the jumbo bag of spinach before it turns slimy.

Europeans survive with very small refrigerators and shop locally most days for their fresh items. Their small refrigerators are easy to clean and do not allow for bulk purchases of perishable items. Some Europeans even live without freezers. The benefits to this particular less-is-more approach are less food waste and simple, healthy meals. Embrace the European way of keeping a bit less food in your home than you're used to, and you'll never have to spend two hours cleaning out your full refrigerator.

In the Life section, you'll learn more about simplifying your meal planning and ways to streamline food preparation. The foundation of your minimalist meals will be a kitchen that contains just the essentials for your favorite quick and healthy meals.

Food Storage Containers

Plastic food containers are not your friends. That drawer full of mismatched lids and cracked sandwich containers isn't helping anyone. It's time to get that space back and never play the "which lid matches which container" game again. Keep just one set of outside-the-home food storage containers per person for lunches. Don't be scared. You already have a food storage solution: pots and dishware. If you're storing leftovers from dinner, let them cool down in the pan or pot, put the lid on, and store it in your refrigerator until you're ready to heat it up for your next meal. One of the secrets to a minimalist life is keeping things simple—that includes meal planning. If you have a serving of spaghetti Bolognese leftover, don't throw it in a container and push it to the back of your refrigerator for retrieval three weeks later when it's growing a new strain of antibiotic. Eat it for your next meal, even if that meal is breakfast. If you don't want to use the pot the meal was cooked in, put the leftover in a bowl or on a plate and cover it with a plate. Yes, this can take up a lot of space, but because you've removed the unneeded food from your refrigerator, you'll have lots of room to store just one plate of leftovers that will be consumed within forty-eight hours.

Remember, among the big benefits of a minimalist life are less distraction and less time and energy wasted on inconsequential choices. By limiting your meal choices, you'll save both time to do other things and mental energy making decisions that you can use for all those wonderful activities you want more of in your life.

Clear Counters

Finally, the goal of your minimalist kitchen: a space for everything. If your kitchen allows, aim to have clutter-free counters. That means no breadbox, no stand mixer, no stacks of clean dishes, and no toaster sitting out. If you're hesitant, just temporarily give it a try. The soothing view of your clean kitchen, with just a flower on the windowsill, will win you over.

Bedrooms

Is your bedroom a calming oasis? Do you easily fall asleep at night? Are the floors clear and is the bed made every morning? Or, like most people, is your bedroom a holding place for unfolded laundry, books you keep meaning to read but never have the time for, and anything that doesn't have a place in your living room?

Decluttering your bedroom should be one of the easiest tasks in your minimalist journey. All you really need in a bedroom is a place to sleep and spot to store your clothes. Unless you live in a studio apartment, you shouldn't be watching television or sewing or using bedroom space for anything other than its intended purpose.

Ditch the Electronics

That's right—remove the television from your bedroom. In fact, remove all electronic gadgets from your bedroom with the exception of an alarm clock. This means your computer, cell phone, tablet, or iPod should all live in another room, preferably your home office or a desk area, overnight. A key to a simple and productive life via minimalism is using your time wisely, and time spent sleeping soundly is an investment in your health and well-being. So, when it's time to sleep, it is best to remove all other distractions.

The television and other screens not only interfere with your biological ability to fall asleep, but they also become distractions during the night if you wake up. Having a light wakeful phase overnight is completely normal and resting calmly in the dark will probably let you return to sleep soon enough. However, if you awake and check your e-mail or turn on a television, you're more likely to have trouble falling back to sleep. For many of us, it's just too tempting to avoid electronics in the middle of the night if they're sitting there on a nightstand. The easiest solution is to save your willpower and simply take the temptation away. When you have an urge to check Twitter or watch television at two in the morning, it will be easily vanquished when you realize you'll have to get out of bed.

Décor

Bedrooms should be peaceful. They should be soothing, not stimulating, and décor should be streamlined. A beautiful bedside lamp, fresh walls in a neutral color, and a bed that you make every morning are enough. Resist having open storage, such as clothing racks or tall, crammed bookshelves. You ideally want to fall asleep without anything visible that will make you think of things you need to do. No errant papers reminding you of bills to pay, no open closets suggesting that you're behind in laundry or alerting you to the dozen items waiting to be picked up at the dry cleaner. Your bedroom should be a sanctuary that makes work and chores a distant thought.

Clothing Storage

Beyond the bed, this room will hold your wardrobe. Again, your wardrobe should easily fit behind closed closet doors and in dresser drawers. If it doesn't, if you've resorted to stacking T-shirts on any available surface and the only thing preventing serious disarray is that most of your clothes are waiting patiently in laundry baskets, you'll want to embrace a minimalist wardrobe.

Wardrobe

Clothing truly deserves a section of its own because most of us have far more than we need. That's why one of the best areas to start your decluttering mission is your wardrobe. Closets can be black holes of money and time. It's so easy to pick up fast fashion and sale items and amass a closet full of pieces that don't suit your body shape or your lifestyle. Most of us wear 20 percent of our clothing 80 percent of the time. So why are you holding on to the jeans that never fit, the stretched-out sweater, and the dated little black dress that you haven't worn in ten years?

Fear. We're fearful that those pants might come back in style, or fit, or we'll eventually find the perfect top/belt/shoes to complete an outfit. The real truth, the one that will set you free to streamline your closet, is that the money you spent on all that clothing is already gone (unless an item still has tags and you kept the receipt). The 80 percent of your closet that you never wear is worth whatever you can get for it at a consignment shop or at a garage sale. So let it go.

If you want to recoup some cash, look to consignment stores or eBay to sell your unwanted items. If you don't think you can get a worthwhile amount selling it, your next step is to donate it. Clean clothing without any rips or stains can be donated to charitable organizations and some even provide tax receipts. If clothing isn't in good enough condition to donate, look for textile recycling drop-off points in your area.

Here's another fear that holds people back from having a minimalist wardrobe: What if people notice you are wearing the same outfit you wore last week? If you reduce your work wardrobe to five outfits that you mix and match and accessorize to create ten different ensembles, no one will ever notice that you wore the same outfit the previous week. They'll instead notice the way you carry yourself in clothes that fit well and compliment your shape. When you let go of the idea that you might someday use some of that unwanted clothing, also let go of the thought that people might notice your small wardrobe. They won't. Most people are far too concerned with their own appearances and lives to keep track of what a colleague wore last week.

Define Your Personal Style

One of the biggest culprits for wardrobe clutter is buying clothing that doesn't suit your personal style. Be it sale signs or fantasies of a different life, many people buy clothing that never makes it out of the closet and still has the tags on it when the owner finally decides to let the item go. It's easy to fall in love with a beautiful silk skirt and impulsively buy it because it's on sale. It's harder to wear that item when it doesn't match anything else in your closet, requires frequent dry cleaning, and is so lightweight that it is only suitable to wear a few months of the year. Clothing isn't meant to be admired on the hanger in your closet; clothing is meant to be worn. So if you have lots of beautiful things that you never wear, either start wearing them or donate them and let someone else show off your good taste.

> **A minimalist wardrobe doesn't mean dressing all in black or wearing the same clothes for days on end.**

Before you start dramatically cutting your wardrobe, take some time to think about your personal style. Most people have a "uniform" in their closet, a combination of clothing and colors that they feel their best in and that they keep coming back to. Look through your closet and consider what you feel good in and are complimented on often. Is it a combination of separates, a color, or one piece of clothing that you always grab when you decide what to wear for the day? This will be the cornerstone of your personal style and help you cull your wardrobe to just what you need.

A minimalist wardrobe doesn't mean dressing all in black or wearing the same clothes for days on end. It does mean cultivating a small closet of flattering outfits that suit your life-style. Building a wardrobe of variations on a signature outfit is timeless and fashionable and, most importantly, helps you feel great in your clothes. If your work look is tailored trousers, a medium-height heel, a blouse or styled top, and a light cardigan, stick with it. If you're a button-down-shirt-with-jeans guy, enjoy how simple it is for you to get dressed in the morning and don't feel pressure to vary your look. Trust that you already know what you feel comfortable in and what looks good on you.

Strategies for Streamlining Your Wardrobe

There are many ways to cull your closet of the unnecessary. Choose one of these three strategies based on what will work for your timeline and habits.

1. Remove anything you haven't worn in a year. This is a quick and effective method for reducing your clothing to just what you really wear. If you have special occasion clothing but haven't had an occasion to wear it recently, keep one outfit for spring and summer and one outfit for winter and fall.

2. Face all your hangers the same way. Every time you wear something turn that hanger the other way. In a few weeks, it will be very clear what items are regularly worn and what items are merely taking up space.

3. Style five or six of your best outfits and get rid of the rest. You should be able to mix and match or accessorize to create a dozen or more variations from your core looks. Keep one set of casual or lounging clothing.

Evening clothes, particularly shoes, should be comfortable enough to wear for up to five hours and to walk short distances. If you trade your heels for flip-flops or bare feet an hour into a party, give those shoes away. There is nothing fashionable or sexy about walking with a limp.

Build a Capsule Wardrobe

The "capsule wardrobe" is a term coined in the 1970s and it refers to a small wardrobe built on interchangeable pieces. All of the items in the wardrobe work as separates and can be transitioned from casualwear to more formalwear with accessories. An example would be a shift dress that works for daytime with a light cardigan and sandals and transitions to evening attire with heels, a chunky necklace, and a Pashmina shoulder wrap. For men, a capsule wardrobe could be office clothing that can mix with more casual pieces outside of work. Think button-down shirts that work with jeans and pullovers that can be worn over a collared shirt to work or over a T-shirt on the weekend. The capsule wardrobe relies on knowing your personal style and owning foundation pieces in neutral colors.

Things to remember when building a capsule wardrobe:

Choose classic shapes and patterns for your base elements. Of-the-moment patterns, colors, and cuts quickly become dated. The crux of the capsule wardrobe is classic fashion pieces in neutral colors. Example: Choose a chambray button-down shirt instead of a bold-patterned or striped shirt. You can bring eye-catching and fun details into your style with accessories.

Pick a color scheme. One or two base colors will make separates interchangeable. Accent colors should be used for accessories and T-shirts or camisoles. Example: A black blazer can be worn with jeans, a black pencil skirt, or a black dress. A camisole, T-shirt, or scarf in a bold color will add variety to the outfits.

Own high-quality clothing. The base of your wardrobe should be timeless and won't need to be replaced as fashions change. Invest in well-made pieces that can be tailored if you gain or lose weight and that will stand up to frequent use. Example: Trousers should be made of a year-round weight of wool and have seams that allow for hemming, taking in, and letting out by a tailor.

Dress for your body shape and complexion. All elements of the capsule wardrobe should flatter your shape, size, and skin tone. Example: Wear an A-line skirt to compliment a small waist and pear shape. If you have a cool complexion, choose accessories in accent colors like silver, royal blue, and navy.

You probably won't need to go out and buy a whole new set of clothes to create a capsule wardrobe. When you downsize your wardrobe, keep those classic, easy-to-wear pieces and build off of them. Make a list of the essentials that you are missing and add them as your budget allows.

Staples of a Capsule Wardrobe

The following lists of basics will help you build a capsule wardrobe. Add accessories with splashes of color and pattern to change the look from day to day.

WOMEN

- One pair of jeans: straight-leg style
- One white button-down shirt
- Six to eight T-shirts and tank tops
- One dress in a neutral color that can transition from work to an evening out
- One cashmere sweater
- One pencil skirt
- One pair of tailored trousers
- One black blazer
- One black cocktail dress in a formal style for weddings and events
- One sundress
- One trench coat

- One pair of flat shoes
- One pair of fashion boots
- One pair of high heels
- Silk scarf
- One over-the-shoulder handbag
- One clutch

MEN

- One pair of jeans
- Six to eight T-shirts
- Four to six button-down shirts
- One pair of trousers
- Pea coat
- Blazer
- Suit
- One pair of sneakers
- Watch
- One pair of dress shoes
- One pair of casual shoes

Adjust these core pieces to suit your lifestyle. If you don't regularly wear a little black dress to work or for an evening out, substitute a piece that you will wear regularly like an extra pair of jeans or a casual dress. If cashmere requires too much upkeep for you, purchase a classically styled sweater that can be machine-washed. With a few such adjustments, you can create a capsule wardrobe that will suit your everyday needs and make you feel more fashionable than a wardrobe four times the size.

Living Room

The living room is meant for relaxing and socializing. It is a space to put up your feet and rest after a day's work. Often, it is also a space to entertain guests. Think of the room's purpose in your life as you decide what should stay and what should go. Do you frequently play the dozen board games you have stored in your massive entertainment unit? Do children play in your living room and are their toys stored there? If you removed everything except what you use 90 percent of the time, could you also remove 50 percent of the furniture? Think critically about how you use your living room space and what those activities require.

> **As you pare down your living room to the essentials, think of it as an exercise in selling your home to yourself.**

If you've sold a home before, you've probably had a real estate agent advise you to remove as much as you can from each room. Simplicity and space are appealing aesthetics for homebuyers. As you pare down your living room to the essentials, think of it as an exercise in selling your home to yourself. Prospective homebuyers want to be able to imagine themselves in a home, and to imagine that their life in that home will be as clutter-free as they see it now. The truth is that no one wants to live in clutter, but most of us do.

A great strategy for going minimalist with your living room is to take everything out and then add pieces back in. If your space allows, empty the room of bookshelves, storage ottomans, wicker baskets full of magazines you haven't had time to read, and whatever else you keep in your living room. Then slowly add pieces back in, first something to sit on, then something to rest a drink on, and finally smaller pieces. What appeals to your eye? What feels relaxing? If you enjoy finally being able to see painted walls, instead of stacked bookcases bursting with paperbacks and old college textbooks that you never really read the first time around, leave it at that. A piece or two of framed art or a small cluster of family photos, and decorating is done.

Delighted with your new beautiful living room, your next question will be, what do I do with all this stuff? All that furniture you bought to hold things that cluttered up the room could be sold or given away. (And the stuff it was holding? That can go too.)

Bathroom

Every medicine cabinet tells a story and every bathroom drawer reveals the inhabitants' truths. The makeup collector with dozens of untouched eye shadows because she mostly wears a bare face. The family prepared for any ailment with four half-filled bottles of the same cough syrup and one empty bottle of ibuprofen. The expired prescription bottles.

The minimalist bathroom should contain only what you need for everyday life. You can get a once-a-year dramatic makeup look at the makeup counter, and any over-the-counter medicine you don't use regularly from a late-night drugstore when necessary. You don't have to be prepared for every scenario that might eventually happen, but you should be prepared for the ones that often do. People get headaches or indigestion, floss regularly, and wear the same mascara, eye shadow, and blush daily. All those one-offs and extras and might-use items can be bought when or if you actually need them.

Bathroom Cabinet Cleanout Plan

Here's how to attack the bathroom: Empty the drawers and cupboards in your bathroom. (Onto the floor is fine because this is going to be a quick job.) First, remove anything that is expired, including old cosmetics, and anything that you no longer use, like those teeth-whitening strips that you tried but didn't like. From your whittled-down collection, reduce even further to just:

- Everyday makeup
- Over-the-counter medicine you use regularly
- Up to one month's supply of all other toiletries
- One container of anything seasonal, like sunscreen

The other piece of clutter in bathrooms: towels. First, remember that you most likely don't live in a hotel or a bed and breakfast. This means two things: You can't leave your wet towel on the floor for housekeeping, and you don't need to impress guests with wicker baskets full of fluffy bath towels. Your bathroom can be beautiful and still contain what you need for a relaxing bath and to get ready for the day.

Dealing with Towels

In a minimalist household, everyone should have just one bath towel and a washcloth, and every bathroom should have one set of hand towels. Bathroom towels may come packaged in sets of three sizes, but most of us rarely use all of them with the same frequency. If you have a guest room or have people stay over regularly, have one or two extra sets of towels.

Within those guidelines, you can even pare down further. For example, if no one in your family uses face-size wash-cloths, get rid of them. If you have sets of towels but don't use each piece of the matching set, get rid of what you never use. Bath towels are large and take up a lot of space. They use a lot of energy when you dry them in a dryer. If you frequently visit the beach or pool, and you can't bear to bring your good towels from home, designate beach towels that can double as guest towels.

How will you get by with just one bath towel per person? You'll hang your towel to dry after every use and wash it once or twice a week. Enforce this towel rule on everyone else in your household too. This is another trick from the Europeans. Though it feels luxurious to have a freshly laundered towel after each shower, it is neither necessary nor does it make your life easier. More towels also mean more storage needed, and more laundry. And all those towels also mean more work: picking up more towels off the floor, adjusting jammed linen closets, and so on.

Beyond the serene bathroom and less laundry, hanging your towel to dry saves time and money: You're doing less laundry, using less laundry detergent, and decreasing your electricity use. It's also better for your back—you'll have fewer big and heavy baskets of wet towels to carry around the house. So the next time you're about to pitch a damp towel into the laundry hamper, consider if you could get one more use out of it if you hung it up to dry.

The Rest of the Bathroom

What else is in your bathroom? Reading material, bath toys, and enough toilet paper to last should there be back-to-back hurricanes for three months? Scale it all back. If you're really going to read those magazines, take the rack to the living room. Keep only enough bath toys to occupy the kids for twenty minutes. Last, only keep whatever toilet paper you can discreetly and easily store. Instead of jamming forty rolls into a too-small cabinet, try buying smaller packages of toilet paper more frequently. You may end up spending a little more money that way, but it's well worth it to have a clean, uncluttered bathroom.

Children's Belongings

Children are often the source of an abundance of household clutter. It starts with an array of swings, swaddles, and soothers in the baby years, transitions to a pile of plastic toys in the toddler years, and then continues to grow and change as the child becomes a teen—sports equipment, electronics, and on and on. Most parents feel there is no way around it: If you have kids, you have clutter.

The truth is, a minimalist can beat clutter even with children. Whether you have one newborn or a full household of six children, four cats, and three dogs, it's possible to beat clutter and live an organized and content life with less stuff. Often parents fall into the trap of thinking that they'll only get their house back (along with their free time) once the kids move out. There is no need to wait until your final child has been sent off to college to declutter your home. You can start now, no matter the ages or number of children in your home.

> **There is no need to wait until your final child has been sent off to college to declutter your home.**

Before you begin decluttering your children's belongings, think about the ages and temperaments of your children and the chronic clutter areas of your home, and then choose the path of least resistance:

- If your children are very young, it will be easiest to declutter without a lot of input from them.

- Older children often actually enjoy decluttering their toys and belongings when they are given responsibility and choice. They get to choose what charity to donate the used toys to and they select their favorites that they want to keep for themselves.

- Teenagers can often be motivated by incentives such as keeping the cash earned from selling their unused goods.

No matter how old your kids are, start small. For most families, decluttering can be a shock, and too much too soon can make a child of any age rebel. Be patient and take your time as you get your children to let go of those things they don't wear or use.

Babies and Preschoolers

The hard truth about clutter for very young children: it's actually parent clutter. We think the baby "needs" a big basket of toys, but really, most children under the age of four can be happily amused with pots and pans from the kitchen, a few well-loved books, and other everyday items already in your home. The closets and drawers that are stuffed with new outfits are for you or Grandma to coo over—not them. No ten-month-old has ever requested multiple teething toys, shape-sorter games, or a dozen stuffed animals. When you accept that a lot of that kid clutter starts with adults, and that most of it isn't necessary for the well-being and happiness of your children, it's easier to find new homes for those things and commit to buying less.

Gear

Too much stuff starts before the first baby even arrives. Expectant parents are inundated with things they *must* buy for the new baby: nursery furniture, layettes of clothing, and all the latest supposedly must-have baby gadgets. Many parents spend more time and money buying things and decorating a nursery than they spend on preparing for the birth or saving for related expenses like maternity or paternity leave. Some families even go so far as to buy a bigger home and a new car before the baby is out of the womb. Ironically, all this buying and stuff, stuff that you need to work more to pay for and spend more of your precious free time tidying up, leaves you with less time to enjoy the new baby.

A hundred years ago, babies slept in dresser drawers, made do with a few outfits and cloth diapers, and were lucky to have just one rattle as a toy. There were no motorized infant swings that promised to lull a baby into a deep sleep. Parents survived with what we would now consider the barest of essentials for a newborn. That's right, they survived and their children thrived anyway. Toddlers learned to walk without any type of push toy or walker. Older babies even learned to eat solid food without a high chair by sitting in their mothers' laps at the dinner table. Parents rocked babies to sleep in their arms rather than in a motorized infant swing that took up a large area of the living room. We can recreate these simpler times now by resisting the impulse to buy every baby-soothing device and gadget we read about in the latest parenting magazines.

With this in mind, re-evaluate your baby gear. What do you really need and use? It's nice to have a safe spot to leave an infant or older baby, either a playpen or something seated, but you really only need one place. The nice thing about baby gear and gadgets is that they are easy to get rid of. Find a family expecting a new baby and they will most likely come to your home and take those big clunky pieces of plastic off your hands tonight. It's funny: You get panicked about needing it all before the baby arrives and then, once the baby is actually here, you can't wait to get rid of that stuff. So say goodbye to some of those big pieces sitting in your living room and reclaim that floor space.

Clothing

Reducing your baby's or toddler's clothing is a great way to create more space and organization in your home and life. With fewer outfits to choose from, you'll be able to get your child dressed faster and have fewer clothes to sort when he or she outgrows things. A nice rule of thumb is to keep just what your child would wear in a week and only outfits that are in good condition and worn often. If you have a lot of special-occasion clothing, just pick your favorite and keep that. As most new parents find out, young kids sometimes outgrow clothing before they even have a chance to wear it once. So send that clothing away. Donate it or sell it and put the proceeds in your child's college fund. A few hundred dollars saved for college tuition will do more for her than a bunch of adorable outfits that she never even wore.

Toys

Toys should be next on your list for a swift and ruthless declutter. Have you ever noticed that the fewer things there are to play with, the better your child plays with them? If two-year-olds only have a choice between a set of blocks and a few toy cars, they will keep themselves entertained for a lot longer than if they are in a playroom with shelves upon shelves of toys. Children become overwhelmed and unable to focus when they have too many choices. With that in mind, zero in on your child's favorites and most basic toys, and get rid of the rest. Even with just the favorites left at home, try using a toy rotation system by dividing the toys into two to three baskets and rotating the basket weekly. This keeps the number of toys in front of your child low, but allows you to keep a select library of toys that challenge your child in different ways.

Finding dual purpose in your things is one of the easiest ways to reduce clutter. Many toys for young children are based on common household goods because that's what babies a few generations ago played with. Stacking or nesting cups for a toddler can be replaced/shared with measuring cups from the kitchen. Make a drum out of a plastic mixing bowl and a wooden spoon. Sometimes the simplest thing that you already own—a parent's water bottle or tennis ball—becomes a favorite toy. Encourage this type of creative and minimalist play in your children.

Books

A nicely stocked bookshelf is a requirement for a healthy childhood, but it need not be an entire bookcase, nor do you need to own every book you read to your kids. Children learn by having stories repeated to them, and most parents find that their kids want the same few books read over and over. So why do you keep those dozens of books that were read only once (or never)? Cull your bookshelf to keep just your favorites and let the library store those books you only read once or twice. This strategy not only saves space, but it saves your family money. To find new favorites, use your local library to test-drive books. When you find a favorite, a book that your children ask for again and again, add it to your permanent collection.

Who Does the Work?

At this age, you should do most of the decluttering. Wait until your children have gone to bed and then quickly cull the toys and books. If you are concerned that your child will miss certain toys, put them in a "hold box" for a few months before donating them. If you're saving things for a possible next baby, keep just the very best items you have and sell or donate the rest. As second-time parents know all too well, there's always a family out there looking to get rid of their baby gear and anything you might need for a second baby can be picked up secondhand for very little money—or often even for free!

Children and Tweens

Once children are school-aged there is a new clutter culprit: keeping up with their peers. Along with homework, school brings more reasons for your children to bring things into the home, such as papers from school and sports equipment, and more influence and pressure to have the latest toys and clothing like their peers. The declutter-by-night tactic that works well for very young children may not be so easily accepted by a seven- or twelve-year-old, who has a precise mental catalog of every action figure and video game in his or her possession. The good news is that by this age with a small amount of assistance from parents, children can declutter on their own.

Getting Kids Involved

Young school-age children need tools and motivation to reduce their stuff, with parents stepping in to provide the structure and rides to the donation center or recycling site. At this age, kids are being exposed to charity drives at school. Donating or selling their rarely used items will help educate them on the environmental and community benefits of owning less stuff. If you can help your children become savvy and environmentally conscious consumers at a young age, while instilling the importance of charitable giving, you'll give them all the tools they need to lead a clutter-free life as adults.

Start the conversation about having fewer things long before you break out the garbage bags and cardboard boxes or even suggest they part with a toy. Here are several ideas for starting a conversation about getting rid of things with a school-aged child:

1. Around her birthday or at Christmas, ask your child to make room for new gifts. This can be as simple as asking her to fill a box with things she no longer likes. The

excitement of the upcoming gifts is often enough to spark a flurry of streamlining. If your child resists, then suggest she wait until after she has received her gifts—for every new item, ask her to donate one item in return.

2. Raise funds or donate items to a favorite cause. If your child is an animal lover, help him sell his old toys, books, and clothes to raise money for an ape habitat or the local zoo. Let your child choose a charity and then set a goal for donating a certain number of boxes or bags of things he isn't using or wearing.

3. Motivate her with assistance for a big purchase. Saving money is a great skill to learn at this age. If your child is saving for a big-ticket item like a bike or gaming device, assist her in selling the things she rarely uses or wears. If the items aren't worth much or you don't have time to list them or hold a garage sale, consider paying your kids to declutter. Tell them for every bag of clothing or box of toys they give away, you will give them a certain number of dollars toward their big purchase.

4. Institute some house rules. This is a great tactic for families struggling to make daily cleanup a routine. Anything left out after bedtime is put in a box for donation. For higher-value items, give a three-strike rule. Your children will quickly realize what things are important enough for them to take care of and what items aren't being used or cherished enough to keep.

5. Set a space or number as a guideline for toys and clothing. Use a toy chest or storage system to set a limit on how many toys your children have. Let them pick through what they own and choose what stays and what goes. The same goes for their clothing. If they can't fit it in their closets or dressers, it has to go.

Play to your children's strengths and interests to get them onboard and excited about living with less stuff. Be sure to share all the benefits they'll get out of having less stuff, such as less time spent cleaning their rooms, the chance to have fewer things of better quality that they will cherish, and the good they will do the environment and community. Every child and family is different, so if at first your child doesn't take to the idea of owning fewer things, try another tactic from the list above.

Teenagers

Modern teenagers are often savvier consumers than their parents. In the age of the Internet and smartphones, teens not only know the cost of clothing and electronics, but they know exactly what they want. Teens know how they want to spend their own money and their parents'. They have more stuff—jeans, shoes, and iPods—than any generation before them. Teens not only have a lot of stuff, but they are also very attached to it as symbols of social status.

How do you get teens to reduce their wardrobes by half and give up one of their electronic devices? Like their younger counterparts, they will need a strategy that motivates them either with the allure of fewer but better things or a call to a cause that means something to them. All of it should be backed up with the phrase that any person of any age will find appealing: Less stuff will make cleaning your room faster and easier.

To get your teens onboard with the family plan to streamline your home, treat them like the adults they are becoming. Budgeting, time management, and taking care of their possessions are all skills they'll need when they leave the nest. Show them how you use those skills as a home manager and ask them to step up and help out. Consult them on the home schedule or meal plans, and then ask them to manage it for a week. As part of their weekly chores, ask them to clean out anything that is expired from the medicine cabinet and pantry. If something of theirs breaks and needs to be repaired, ask them to split the cost with you by either selling something they own or using their own funds from an allowance or job. These are small steps to help them grasp how much work it takes to manage a household that is low on time and money and high on stuff.

Once your teen has had a taste of what it takes to keep your house running, talk to him or her about why you're getting rid of things and buying less. Now is the time to get into the nuts and bolts of how your family, and your teen specifically, will benefit from using minimalism to have a more organized home, more money, and more time. Talk to him or her about what you'll be doing with these savings: you'll have more time and more free cash for family vacations and to put toward college education, and with less stuff in the home there will be less to clean and maintain, so chores will be easier.

Here are more ideas for projects to get your teens to reduce what they own and spend:

1. Trust your teen to transition his wardrobe to the next season by himself. Give him the responsibility of deciding what clothes are in good enough condition to resell, what should be donated, and what, if anything, should be saved for a younger sibling.

2. Do a leave-for-college "test run." Ask your teen to pack up her room as if she were moving to college. Remind her of the space she will likely be moving into: a shared dorm room with small closets, one bookshelf, and a single bed. This can be a great way to segue into keeping just her most beloved and well-used items and donating what she has outgrown or rarely uses.

3. Take a family trip to the garbage dump. Seeing how much waste households produce can be a strong motivator for more thoughtful consumerism and less waste.

Teaching your teen how to live with fewer things will not only enhance your family life and home; it will give you peace of mind when you send your child off into the world. Wouldn't it be great to know that your own children will never fill a basement with old college textbooks and boxes of outdated clothing? Consider the time and energy spent encouraging your teens to declutter as an investment in their future financial and emotional well-being.

Storing Children's Hand-Me-Downs

Are you storing clothing, toys, and books for that yet-to-be-conceived next baby? Do you have your eleven-year-old's winter clothes from last year packed away with the idea that your six-year-old will eventually wear them? Storing clothes for "someday" often leaves you with big clutter problems today. The boxes and storage containers pile up as the years go by. Often, the clothes from one child never get worn by the next because they fit in the wrong season or the child has very different tastes than his or her older sibling.

Sure, you can save some cash by using hand-me-downs, but you can also lose money. Items that wait for years in storage can become moldy from damp conditions or get moth-eaten. If the fashions are of-the-minute, they may look outdated by the time they are ready for the next child. Sometimes you're so busy you forget what you have packed away, and that snowsuit you saved for two years ends up going to a neighbor because you bought a new one before checking what you had in storage.

Unless you can pass clothing directly from one child to the next to wear, only keep your best pieces. If you used the advice in this section to scale back your kid's clothing to a week's worth, you are probably close to having just what you can easily store for another child. Set a goal for hand-me-downs by limiting your storage to a number of outfits per size. For babies, it might mean anywhere from six to a dozen onesies or sleepers and for a seven-year-old it might mean four bottoms and eight tops. Kids' clothing is easy enough to come by secondhand if you need to fill out a younger child's wardrobe.

> ## Set a goal for hand-me-downs by limiting your storage to a number of outfits per size.

More radical and storage-scant parents should consider not storing any clothes at all. Yes, even if you have children a few years apart, think about the space, time, and stress you would save if instead of storing old clothes you sold them on consignment instead. A good children's consignment clothing store can act like a clothing library for families. Consign pieces as children grow out of them and then use store credit to purchase secondhand for the next child. Any wardrobe gaps can be filled by suggesting clothing as birthday or holiday gifts from grandparents and family. This is a bold move, but it can free a family from a lot of stress and clutter.

Tip: don't delve into those boxes of stored clothing until you have a few hours on hand and you've already made a plan and know when and where the unneeded clothing will be sent. Clothes often conjure a lot of memories, so be prepared to take a trip down memory lane as you decide what should stay and what should go.

Home Office

Imagine sitting at a desk with nothing on it but your computer. No mug of pens, stack of bills, or errant paper clips hiding under your keyboard. You sit down to tackle a task—say, paying bills online or checking in on a work project—and your focus is sharp. Instead of being distracted by the things cluttering your work area, you are able to quickly and efficiently get your work done. Thirty minutes later, you're turning your computer off and using the rest of your weekend or evening for the fun and leisure you deserve.

Unfortunately, this scenario doesn't happen for most of us. The home office you created, the one that was going to help you get more done, usually turns into a den for anything you can't fit in the rest of your home. "Home office" usually means home gym/extra closet/guest room/storage room. The sanctuary you created to write your novel is the first thing to go when you have too much stuff.

If you've decluttered your home in the order listed in this book, you should now have a clear vision of what you want to keep in your home. With these new eyes, you'll be able to spot and remove the nonessentials from your home office. The seasonal clothing that you stored in the closet can be pared down and put where it belongs (in your bedroom). If the office truly is the best place for your treadmill, and you're actually using the treadmill frequently, keep it. The goal is to work with the space you have to facilitate the truly important things in your life.

Getting Rid of Paper Clutter

Paper is a big clutter culprit in home offices. We'll work on reducing incoming paper and creating an effortless system to deal with all the bills and statements later, in the Life section. For now, as you discover what your home office really looks like without all that stuff, file all your paper clutter into a box. Right now focus on the things that are already covering your desk, chair, and in some cases, the floor. Once all your paper clutter is in one spot, sort it into four piles: shred, recycle, file, and action.

Shred

Anything with personal or sensitive information on it should be shredded. Don't have a paper shredder? Before you run out and buy one, try to source some alternative shredding methods:

- Some companies allow employees to shred personal documents at work.

- Check with your local office-supply or copy shop to see if they offer confidential shredding services.

- If you compost kitchen waste, you can "shred" paper by adding it into your compost system.

It's very important to dispose of sensitive documents properly to avoid things like identity theft, so find a method that works for you and that you can do regularly.

File

Next, take your "file" pile and cull the papers again. Put some fresh eyes on all that paper and think about your home filing system and how often you use it. It's smart to have a paper copy of your mortgage or life-insurance policy filed away, but you don't really need the receipt for a blender you bought three years ago. One main culprit of paper clutter is receipts and statements that you don't really need. If your utility companies provide account information online, you can shred statements or sign up for paperless billing or online-only statements.

This is your chance to reduce your home filing system to just the essentials: birth certificates, legal documents, and warranties for large appliances. Here's a list of things you might be holding onto in a file cabinet that you can get rid of:

- **Appliance manuals.** Most manuals are available online and you can search for videos detailing how to fix, reset, or operate the appliance. If you're not comfortable being without a paper manual, reduce the size of it by cutting out any sections that are in a foreign language.

- **Receipts.** If you're thinking about returning an item, keep the receipt in your wallet to remind yourself to return it within the store's return policy timeframe. Set a cut-off price for keeping receipts, such as anything over $50. If you paid for something with a credit card, often a credit card statement listing the purchase can act as a receipt. Again, instead of keeping every credit-card statement use online services to print a statement when you need it.

- **Statements.** Why are you keeping that phone bill from three years ago? Unless it is required for work, shred it.

Saving every bank, utility, credit card, and phone statement for a household will exponentially increase the amount of filing space needed. In this age of electronic statements and storage, you don't need to keep as many paper files. Again, if you haven't already done so, sign up for paperless statements and familiarize yourself with each bank's and company's online customer service portal.

Your Computer

This is a great opportunity to clean up the desktop of your computer. If you download files and pictures and leave them directly on the desktop of your computer, you probably can barely find what you need on your desktop. Instead, make folders and store files in an organized way. You want your computer to look and feel as peaceful and centered as the room you are working in.

Non-Home-Office Belongings

If your home office has turned into a storage or multi-purpose room, recommit to making it a space for work. This means making space in your bedroom closet for the extra clothes you store in the office closet, taking that appliance you need to repair to the repair shop, and finding a new home for, or donating, anything else that isn't related to your home office. A home office space is meant just for that: working from home.

Décor

Now that you've unearthed your desk and dramatically reduced the amount of paper in your home office, it's time to create a peaceful workspace. Choose up to three of your favorite décor pieces for your desk and dust and display them. A framed photo, a paperweight, and a few pens are enough. If you have a pin board, remove anything that isn't recent or urgent.

Is Your Home Office Even Necessary?

Now that you've restored order to your home office, ask yourself, do I really need a dedicated room for a home office? With digital storage solutions, you can easily contain household documents in a small file cabinet. Online calendars, wireless Internet, wireless printing, and other office solutions mean you need less physical space and fewer things for home offices. If you've always wanted more space in your home, consider giving up the home office. Work can be done from the dining room table if you have a laptop, and a wireless printer can be stored almost anywhere in your house. That small paper file system could be stored in any communal room in the home. A dedicated home office isn't always a necessity with the ability to work on a laptop from almost anywhere.

Maintenance

You've peeled back the layers of your home and left yourself with a tidy space that reflects your life and loves. You've put the work in and can now enjoy the many rewards. Your home is now easy to clean and to keep tidy. You can finally find things when you need them and you can relax with all that clutter gone. Enjoy your newfound space and freedom.

To keep the clutter at bay long-term, you'll need to do two things:

1. Be discerning about what you bring into your home.

2. Regularly review what's in your home and if it is still serving a purpose.

Ideally, you should declutter your home with the seasons. As you put your summer clothing away, donate anything you didn't wear that year. Take a quick tour of the rest of your home for things that you're no longer using and that can be given to someone who will use and enjoy them. You've done the heavy lifting—but, like a dieter who is now in maintenance mode, you'll need to keep your new shape by regularly weighing in with your possessions.

A Final Word

It can be overwhelming to realize the amount of things in your home that you're not using—not only because they've been untouched for months and years, but because you spent your hard-earned dollars on them. And those dollars equal time. Every misguided purchase at the mall is equal to hours at your job. For some people the amount of clutter they clear from their homes can equal a good chunk of their annual salaries.

Don't mentally beat yourself up for mistakes you made in the past. The money is spent, and if you are able to recoup a fraction of it by reselling some items, you've done well. Keeping those things you never wear or use just wastes *more* of your time, and time is money.

> ## Don't mentally beat yourself up for mistakes you made in the past.

The good news is that you don't have to waste your earnings anymore. From this day forward you can spend thoughtfully and resist the siren song of sales. From this day forward you can invest your money and space and time in the things you love and use. So leave the past and your misspent dollars behind and get ready to start a new chapter in your spending life. In the Money section of this book, you'll learn how to use minimalism in your financial life to save more and redefine your relationship with the almighty buck.

Lastly, congratulations. You've decluttered your home and created a beautiful space to live, work, and play in. Enjoy!

Work

" Fear less, hope more; eat less, chew more; whine less, breathe more; talk less, say more; love more, and all good things will be yours. "

—Swedish proverb

The sixty-hour workweek used to be reserved for lawyers and medical students. Today, with smartphone in hand, most people on a salaried wage work far more than the forty-hour-a-week company policy. Factor in a meager week or two of vacation time and most people really do live attached at the hip to the office. Balancing personal time with work life has never been harder.

Whether you work to live or live to work, minimalism can help you define your goals, work efficiently, and balance your time at and away from the office. The minimalist path to work success can mean working less, finding a new job, or even changing careers. Your choice and path will be unique to you and your goals and dreams. If you're burned out by a long commute, explore the idea of shifting where you work, or even where you live, to take back weeks of your time. Unfulfilled by your current role? Minimalism will help you find your passion and translate it into a career.

Think big. Do you want to go back to school? Apprentice in a new field? Cut down your work hours so you can finish that great American novel you started years ago? Do you want to work in the nonprofit sector? Do you want to work overseas? No change is too small, no goal too big.

Just as minimalism can transform your home and finances, it can also change your work life. You can Do Less and be more efficient, happier, productive, and successful. In this section of the book, we'll explore all of the different routes you can take to build a more productive work life.

Work Smarter

Parkinson's law of triviality states that we put time into making a decision in inverse proportion to the importance of the decision. In 1957, C. Northcote Parkinson, a British author, used bike sheds and atomic reactors to show how organizations spend time on things in inverse proportion to their complexity and cost. He explained how a committee would debate the merits, cost, and design of a bike shed for hours because it is something most people would have some experience with, or have enough knowledge of, to form an opinion on. The debate would take a lot of time and the organization would deliberate at great length on trivial details and small costs. In comparison, a similar debate about an atomic reactor wouldn't occur that way, because those who work on it have such specialized knowledge and skill that there is no need for anyone to contribute to the discussion or debate in a trivial way. The bottom line: the more complex and specialized the matter, the less room there is for triviality.

Most workplaces are rife with the trivial. Meetings run late because someone wants to contribute a long-winded case on something small that has little to no impact on a project. In deference to good manners, we let our coworker prattle on while hundreds of dollars of man-hours disappear as colleagues sit idle, waiting for him or her to finish.

Clutter doesn't begin and end in our homes. The workplace is just as much a culprit when it comes to stealing time and money as our homes and hobbies are. Many of us take work home with us in the evening, come into work on weekends, and check in on our jobs while on vacation. We work longer hours than we need to and we don't have an improved product or great volume of work to show for it.

Minimalism can help you work less, not only by reducing your income needs, but also by helping you work smarter. Working smarter doesn't necessarily mean working harder—

it means working more efficiently. The minimalist approach to work means assessing your own work style and the work culture and norms in your office, and then adjusting how and when you work for success. Be open to the idea that your actual workplace values—the ones that are used day to day rather than the ones on the company mission statement—may be slightly outside of conventional norms and practices. (Work culture and the unique skills and tastes of coworkers and management often override the formal value statement in an employee handbook.)

What Does Your Workplace Value?

You're going to realign your work based on the culture of your workplace in a few simple steps. You're going to change how and when you work to suit the optics of your office. You're going to work more efficiently and when it will be noticed so that you can work less when it won't be noticed and spend less time chained to your desk. Get ready to rethink how, when, and where you work.

In order to figure out what your workplace values, ask yourself some questions about what gets people ahead.

- Is it the early bird who gets the kudos from management? Do you see your coworker who regularly sends early-morning and late-night e-mails rising to the top?

- Is it the person who fervently argues in a meeting and shows that she's not afraid of being the lone dissenter who gets the promotion?

- Is high output, no matter the quality, rewarded?

- Look at your colleagues who are consistently praised and rewarded. What do they have in common?

Many workplaces give lip service to traditional measures of performance like punctuality, volume, and quality of work and *actually* reward a completely different set of skills and traits. Unearth what those are at your workplace.

Reconsider When You Work

What time does your workday start? What about your colleagues'? Is there someone who typically arrives fifteen to thirty minutes later than everyone else? Everyone else might make note of it, but does management? Is that two and a half hours a week that your colleague isn't in the office hurting his or her career? If you had an extra two and a half hours a week to do with as you please, what would you do?

Forget about what the conventional working hours are and look at what the actual ones are in your workplace. If the manager values people who stay until six, even if they arrived an hour later than everyone else, make that work for you. You can do this by coming in later, taking a longer lunch and using some of that time to run personal errands, or leaving early and logging back onto work e-mail when you get home. You don't have to put in a lot of work, merely send a few e-mails or finish a small item to send the message that, like everyone else, you worked until six. Adjusting when you work to fit the hours valued by your employer will not only raise your profile at work, but it will also allow you to work less at other times.

Let go of the idea that the workday must be nine to five. Many successful people are night owls and others work best in short concentrated bursts of time. If you are in tune with how and when you work best, adjust your work schedule to those hours while being mindful of the necessities of your workplace. If you prefer to come to work later after a leisurely morning at home, but there is an unspoken rule that 8:30 A.M. is the general start time, hold back some e-mails you might send at night and instead send them first thing in the morning while you are still at home. Get the work done, but present it in a timeline that suits your employer or manager.

Tip: want to take a longer lunch hour? Leave your desk "un-tidied" with some carefully placed paperwork that works as desk camouflage. Give the appearance that you've just stepped away from your desk to use the toilet or discuss something with a colleague, even if you're actually at the gym for a forty-minute spin class.

Use Your Ultradian Rhythm to Work More Efficiently

Do you struggle to get the big work done at your job? Are you often mired down with administrative tasks and too busy to do the really important work that will advance your career and impress your manager? Most of us have to leave the distractions of the workplace, the water-cooler talk, the incessant e-mails, to get our critical work done. Big deadlines often mean taking work home with us or coming in on weekends. These sixty-hour workweeks burn us out physically and mentally and sap our time and energy for any other pursuits.

In these busy workplace cultures, it's important to tap into your natural rhythms to be at your most productive when it counts. "Ultradian rhythms" are those natural cycles that happen in a human body in a twenty-four-hour cycle and include your patterns of sleep, appetite, and even frequency of blinking. You want to harness these rhythms and assign your most important work to certain time periods.

The following is a sample schedule for a workday with timed intervals during which you will do your most important and challenging work. Remember, we all have our own internal rhythms and external schedule demands. Tailor this schedule to your own needs. If you're an early riser, you may even want to put a work interval in as soon as you wake up. Some of us work best just out of bed, clad in pajamas and sitting in our home offices. If you work best in the late afternoon to evening, stagger your work intervals to start once you have been in the office for two to three hours.

Always take note of when your attention wanders and for what reason. Are you hungry, tired, or bored? You'll be able to train yourself to work up to longer sessions, but always read your own physical and mental cues for when you need a break. It's much better to grab a glass of water, respond to a few non-stressful e-mails, and reset yourself mentally than to stare blankly at a screen as the clock ticks on.

After a few weeks of working within a schedule and keeping performance notes on yourself, you'll know what your optimal time is to break for lunch, take a walk around the office, or move on to less demanding work.

SAMPLE WORK DAY USING ULTRADIAN RHYTHMS

8:00–10:00 A.M.: First work interval. Put your phone on silent, ignore your e-mail, and tackle those tough tasks and projects.

10:30–11:30 A.M.: Administrative tasks, coffee break, meetings. Take a walk around the office and spend a few minutes socializing with your coworkers; respond to any urgent e-mails.

11:30–1:00 P.M.: Second work interval. Again, avoid distractions and focus on tough projects that require your complete attention. Resist checking your e-mail and if possible let any phone calls go to voicemail.

1:00–2:00 P.M.: Lunch. Take a real break from work and the office and eat your lunch outside or in a room with a nice view. Only eat lunch at your desk while doing light work if you are truly in a time crunch. Your lunch hour should be rejuvenating and prime you for your third work interval.

2:00–3:30 P.M.: Third work interval. Final focused work interval of the day.

3:30–4:00 P.M.: Break, walk, socialize. As your colleagues hit their own fatigue points of the day, you will naturally switch into a casual and less focused mode. Enjoy it!

4:00–5:00 P.M.: Wrap up your work for the day. This is an ideal time to send your work to colleagues for review or response. If they are able to respond before the end of the workday, use their feedback to create notes that you will review and work from the next morning. Respond to e-mails and voicemails, enter expenses, and do any other tasks required to clear your virtual and physical desk for the day.

This sample schedule can be a starting point for some people or an end goal for others. We all have different capacities for focused work and we all work at different speeds. If you struggle with highly focused work, break down your workday into two or three evenly spaced ninety- to 120-minute segments to start. These cycles should be used for demanding work that requires a high level of focus. This is not a time to answer e-mails or idly surf the human resources section of the company intranet. These short cycles are times to create or edit documents or projects or brainstorm for a new initiative. Close your e-mail program, turn your phone to silent, and set your messenger status to do not disturb.

As you begin working in this way, try starting with a shorter work cycle of thirty to sixty minutes. If you are used to checking your e-mail every five minutes or frequently being interrupted by coworkers, it will take a few sessions for you to get your focus skills back and to eliminate distractions during these relatively short bursts of work. Your busywork—the stuff that you can do while also keeping an eye on a basketball game on television or while chatting with a colleague—can be done outside of your focused work cycles. Using these work cycles to be more productive during your workday will make you more efficient and allow you to leave your work at the office every night instead of taking it home with you.

The Law of Diminishing Returns

Once you've tapped into your ultradian rhythms, you will become aware when you hit a point of diminishing returns at work. We all have limits to how long we can work in a focused and productive way, and when we work beyond that limit, we make mistakes and the quality of our work suffers. A thirty-minute task stretches into two hours because we start surfing the web or writing personal e-mails. If you want to work more efficiently, you need to recognize your threshold for work and stop or change your work when you hit that threshold.

In practical application, recognizing the law of diminishing returns in your work can mean:

- Saying no to working after a certain time in the evening

- Building rejuvenating breaks into your day

- Taking your lunch break away from your desk and going for a brisk walk outside before returning to work

- Shutting off your work computer in the evening and doing something that engages you a different way, such as exercising or enjoying a hobby

These types of breaks will help you reset so that when you return to work, whether it's thirty minutes later or fourteen hours later, you are ready for focused and highly productive work.

Work Less

We're working longer hours than ever before. Many of us aren't even taking vacations. The toll on our health and relationships from these long hours is evident. We're tired and stressed out, and although we can blame work culture and the mobile and 24/7 nature of work today, there *is* a way out. There is a way to work less and live more—it's minimalism.

Why are we working so much? During her years helping people through their final weeks of life, hospice nurse Bronnie Ware observed several common regrets people had about what they wished they had done more of or less of in their lives. She chronicled them in her memoir, *The Top Five Regrets of the Dying: A Life Transformed by the Dearly Departing.* A big regret of the dying was working too much. As people reflected on how they'd lived their lives, it became clear that working long hours had kept them from the people they loved and the pastimes that nourished their souls.

Obviously, the long hours and sparse vacation time aren't serving you well. But how do you change things? How do you reduce your work hours or even days? Is it really possible to start taking alternate Fridays off or to negotiate working from home or even ask for unpaid leave? Yes. If your goal is to work less so you can have more personal time, you need to realign your work hours to give you more time for those things you really value. With some small easy steps, you can start the process of working less and enjoying life more.

Figure Out Where You Could Cut Work-Related Expenses

The first answer is to reduce your need for the paycheck. The Money section of this book will give you ideas for cutting your bills, and in the Home section, you learned how to live well by owning and spending less. Revisit your expenses before you make your plan for reducing work hours or taking extra leave. Are there a few more things you can do without if you're spending less time in the office? There are inherent savings to working less, such as:

- Reduced commuting costs

- Less wear on work clothing

- Less money spent on daycare

- Less money spent on takeout food

- Less money spent on hiring others to do home services, such as cleaning or repairs, because you don't have the time do them yourself

Make a list of all those things you regularly spend money on that you could eliminate or reduce if you worked less.

Learn to Say No

Are you always behind at work? Do you take on more responsibility and projects than you have time for? If the root of your long hours at the office is an unrealistic workload, it is time to learn to say no. It is time to sit down with your manager and outline all the work you are currently responsible for and how much of it can be realistically done by one person in the hours described in the company policy. Many of us find ourselves working evenings and weekends because we say yes to every request that comes our way and we take on far more than is in our job description.

If you find it difficult to say no, start equating new projects and tasks with what will suffer in your personal life. Saying yes to extra work will mean less sleep, less time with your loved ones, and less time for those things you love to do. Saying yes to extra work means saying yes to more stress, and more stress is bad for your health and can take years off your life. Is it worth it? Start asking yourself that before you accept a new project.

Change Your Hours or Work from Home

Changing your work hours and working from home are two simple ways to work less. If you have a long commute that doubles during rush hour, request an earlier or later start so that you can reduce your driving time to increase your living time. Ideally this shift in work hours plays into your natural strengths, such as an early start if you're a morning person, or a later start if one of your goals is to have a relaxed morning of personal time before work.

An important piece to remember when negotiating different working arrangements and schedules is that a lot of employers don't have experience with these requests. If anything, people want to work *more* these days. You may be a maverick in the company! For the arrangement to be successful and beneficial for both you and your employer, you should approach it gradually and thoughtfully.

At first, you may want to ask for something small, like working from home two days a month. If you have a thirty-minute commute to work, this change alone can give you the equivalent of three extra days off a year with no loss of salary. In addition to that extra time, you'll also save on commuting costs. Although it might seem frustrating to start with such a small request, there are still big lifestyle and financial gains to be made with just a small change in your work arrangements.

When you ask to work from home two days a month, offer a trial basis of three months. This is especially important if flexible work arrangements aren't common at your workplace. The goal of this trial period is to impress your manager with the benefits to the company so that he or she is open to other flexible work arrangements down the road. Use the ideas in the Work Smarter section to be very productive during the trial period of your new work schedule. A flexible work arrangement hinges on employer/employee trust, so treat your new privileges with the same professionalism you would the rest of your job. If you successfully negotiate working from home, resist taking a work-at-home day outside of the set schedule. This respect for the freedom you are being given will go a long way in creating the trust needed for successful flexible work arrangements.

Reduce Work Hours

Reducing work hours is the next obvious step to working less. One relatively easy change if you work shifts is to ask to reduce your hours and, in the interim, offer one of your shifts to a coworker who needs extra money. (Many people are looking to work more, not less, because they have bills to pay and so much stuff they want to buy. When you, however, decide to Do Less, you are freeing yourself of that all-consuming need to work more and more.)

If you are in a salaried position, rather than hourly or shift work, take a hard look at your workload:

- Can your job truly be done in four days instead of five without the loss of hours impacting the quality of your work?

- Could you ask to work four longer days instead of five traditional workdays?

- Could you telecommute one day a week?

- If your job can't be condensed, think of tasks that could easily be shared or shifted to a coworker or perhaps into a new role.

- Keep your eyes and ears open for colleagues who are also looking for flexible work arrangements or anyone eager to take on more responsibility and projects. A colleague interested in working fewer hours could become a valuable ally for job sharing.

Strategies for Negotiating
with Your Company

When you sit down to discuss your desired work arrangement with your manager, come prepared with a list of the benefits to the employer rather than the benefits to yourself. You'll need to prove that working less is in the company's favor, rather than just part of your own plan to create more time for yourself.

If at first you don't succeed in reducing your work hours, be patient. It may not be the right time for your employer, but you can still use the ideas in the Work Smarter section to leave your work at work instead of taking it home at night. Continue to build a case for flexible work arrangements, and when it's time for your next performance review, ask again for a trial period to work less or work from home.

If work flexibility is completely unavailable, consider looking for a new job. More and more information shows that flexible work arrangements benefit employers as much as they benefit employees. Unless you're on the cusp of retirement, there is no reason not to look for work arrangements that fit your new simplified lifestyle. Keep your eyes and ears open for friends and acquaintances who have flexible work. Good jobs are often found person-to-person rather than in traditional advertisements or listings.

Rethink Retirement

Retirement might not be the panacea or enticing finish line people envisioned years ago. Previous generations of retirees benefited from good pensions, decades of saving when credit was scarce and consumerism far less rampant, and jobs that they left at the office each night rather than carried around with them in their pockets. The people currently living well in retirement had far more work-life balance in their careers than most of us do today.

Live Like You're Retired *Now!*

The long hours, stress, and sitting at our desks and in cars for most of the day are actually eroding our ability to enjoy our golden years. We're not putting the energy into our health and wellness because we're so busy working. And if we don't take care of our health now, we'll face a shocking decline in the quality of our lives as we hurtle into old age. The visions of annual cruises and summers golfing will be replaced by the reality of medical appointments and bills. The active retirement life we dreamed of will evaporate under the weight of our poor health and limited mobility.

If all that sounds very depressing, don't despair. It's never too late to start living better, no matter how old you are. It's yet another reason to streamline your home and working life with minimalism. To enjoy many tomorrows, you need to take care of yourself today. Do not deceive yourself into thinking you will get into shape or start eating better or reduce your stress when the pace of life is a bit slower. Start your wellness plan—your working less, doing less, and living more plan—*today* if you want to enjoy your golden years.

Besides, why wait for retirement to start enjoying your life? Embrace minimalism, and you can restart that hobby, reconnect with family, or finally learn another language now, not in retirement. Live a vibrant life every day of your life. Let go of the idea that retirement will be a line in the sand or that it's when you'll finally do the things you've been putting off for years because you're too busy. You can have a wonderful work-life balance before retirement if you simplify and use the tenets of minimalism to reduce your income needs. Enjoy your life more by having less no matter what stage of your work life you are in: just starting out, mid-career, or retirement.

The Financial Piece

We all need money to retire, and yet, if we spend forty years working ourselves to the bone, we won't be able to enjoy those golden years. The answer to this conundrum is to be flexible and, again, align life with your values now. You'll have to live differently now if you want to live well during retirement. Here are several ideas for restructuring your work and retirement plans:

- Work less now but work longer. Push retirement back indefinitely and work less now so that you can enjoy life both now and down the line. Working part-time into your golden age will keep your mind sharp and can actually improve the quality of your retirement life. If you love your career, this can be a great way to slowly transition into not working. Working part-time in retirement could also be a chance to explore a new interest by taking on an entry-level job in a new industry or turning a hobby into a part-time job.

- Work less now and reduce your cost of living. With your new minimalist attitude about what you need to be happy, you can cut your expenses and still stay on track for retirement. In fact, you may even hit retirement age earlier because you'll need less money to live off of later in life.

- Take mini-retirements from work. Many employers offer sabbatical programs, allowing you to take unpaid leave. Some employers even have options to take a salary reduction for several years and then take a paid sabbatical. Mini-retirements could mean anything from taking a few extra weeks of unpaid vacation time annually to taking a full year away from the office. If you are in a very secure industry with lots of job availability, a mini-retirement could mean quitting your job and taking three months off before finding a new job.

Do Work That You Love

For some us a paycheck, nice coworkers, and a desk near a window are enough to make the workweek enjoyable. We like our jobs, but they aren't passions. For others, a job is not just a job but also something that allows us to express ourselves, pursue lofty goals, and work very hard. If you are in a job that you don't like and you yearn not to work less or retire early, but to do something you truly love and that excites you, this next section is for you. Life is too short to spend forty or more hours a week at a job you really hate when you have dreams and ambitions for something bigger. So if you're itching to get out and start a business or make a hard right in your career, think minimalism! It helps to remind yourself that nothing bought in a store can bring the same happiness as following your dreams.

Find Your Dream Job

What was your dream job from childhood? Some of us wanted to be firefighters or astronauts or ballerinas. As we got older those dreams faded, or reality set in. We quit ballet in third grade or we realized only a few people become astronauts and we weren't going to be one of them. We saw that not every job was illustrated in a Richard Scarry book. Some of us replaced these dreams with more practical goals, but some of us never replaced them at all and merely fell into a job and career. The first place that hired us out of high school or college dictated that we would manage a retail clothing store (even though we weren't that enthused about men's fashion) or eventually become an IT project manager (because the job prospects looked promising). Our dreams became just that, dreams instead of goals, and we resigned ourselves to the jobs and industries we fell into or chose because they were safe.

Some people know just what job they'd love to do. If you don't, now is the time to explore different career possibilities. Ask yourself questions about what appeals to your interests and works to your strengths. Do you like working with and for people, or do you prefer working independently with infrequent interaction with colleagues or customers? Meeting with a career counselor or taking a personality test like Myers-Briggs can help you narrow in on your ideal career.

You may already have an idea of the work you would love to do, but you can't see how to make it happen. Your fourth-grade dream was to be a doctor, but now you work in finance and still have regrets about not pursuing medical school. Changing careers is a daunting task as you get older. Getting into medical school in your thirties or forties, though not impossible, is hugely challenging. After all, the realities of a career U-turn don't mesh well with life realities such as college payments or retirement plans.

Now that you've seen that you can live well and simply on a fraction of the money you once thought you needed, however, maybe you *can* take that big risk and completely change careers. The insurance broker can go back to school and become a medical technician. The administrative assistant can become a grade-school teacher. We've talked about living simply and reducing your cost of living, and there are dozens of ideas in this book to reduce your expenses so that you can make a career change. If that is your unfulfilled dream, go after it. It make take a few years of planning and saving before it becomes a reality, but if it truly is your passion, it will be well worth the effort.

If you're itching to change jobs but don't want to go back to school, consider a career shift rather than a 180-degree change. Perhaps you could still do your job, but for a different industry. You could work in finance for a hospital or a group practice, or work for a nonprofit that provides medical services overseas. If you manage a restaurant but always dreamed of working for a professional sports team, you could manage food concessions at a ballpark. There are ways to make your dream job a reality without starting from scratch or spending a ton of money on a new degree.

Consider Volunteer Work

Another option is to work in your dream field as a hobby. We'll talk more about using your time wisely and with intention in the Life section of this book, but for now consider, if you had the time, could you volunteer or work part-time? The answer to your dream job quest may not be a new day job, but evenings or weekends spent volunteering in a field related to your dream job—instead of in front of the television or out shopping.

> **Although some of your childhood dreams may no longer be a reality, achieving something close to them is always possible.**

If you always wanted to be a veterinarian, you could work with animals in some way, perhaps volunteer at an animal shelter or foster puppies before they are trained as Seeing Eye dogs. You could start a dog-walking business or a weekend kennel service. Although some of your childhood dreams may no longer be a reality, achieving something close to them is always possible. The closet journalist can cover recreational league basketball for the local paper and the amateur baker can start a small weekends-only cupcake business. Fulfilling an interest or passion part-time, with the safety net of a bill-paying nine-to-five job, is a great way to explore a possible new career.

Transition to a New Career

For some of us, the childhood fantasy of being a professional athlete has been replaced by a more burning desire to go back to school or become our own boss. You might have very real and possible goals, ones that you have already studied or created business plans for, but you can't make the big leap or really commit to them because of your commitments at home, your need for a paycheck, or your lack of startup money. Minimalism to the rescue: if you have your heart set on another career or starting your own business, minimalism can help you make those plans a reality.

Starting your own business or switching careers isn't common because both of these endeavors are incredibly difficult. If it were easy, everyone would be opening a restaurant, turning that sewing hobby into an online business, or taking two years out of the workforce to go back to school and become a dental hygienist. Many people have these ambitions, but few actually make the leap to that new career or building that business simply because it requires a lot of time, money, and effort.

These goals can be achieved, but you must break through two hurdles first: reduce your cost of living and increase available time. Here's how minimalism can help you jump those hurdles:

- The Home section gave you ideas for decluttering so you can live with less in a smaller space—thus freeing up time you used to spend cleaning and doing maintenance on your home.

- The Life section will help you create more time by reprioritizing your activities.

- The Money section will give you ideas for bill cutting and getting out of debt.

To give this new business or career your best shot, you'll need to trim your finances and even your social life. Minimalism can be a jumping-off point for your plan and will help transition you from dreams to reality.

When you want to career transition, it is imperative that you realize that you'll have to put the work in before life gets easier and simpler. You'll need to live simply and without a lot of extras while you pursue your passion. You'll need to save some of those hours you would spend out with friends for attending classes, studying, or building your business. If this business or new career is your true passion, it shouldn't be difficult to spend a weekend studying, working on a business plan, or answering customer e-mails. As Confucius said, "choose a job you love and you will never have to work a day in your life." Although you might have to drum up some enthusiasm for the more mundane tasks of your new business, such as bookkeeping, the day-to-day of it should be something you're excited about and would do for free if you could. This burning passion for the job will be what sustains you while you temporarily work your day job on top of your new business.

When to Make the Leap

The more tenets of minimalism you can embrace, the faster you'll reach the critical requirements to leave your day job. If you're building a business or freelance career, you'll need a lot less income, and you might be able to leave your day job sooner, if you have a small mortgage or very little rent to pay. Set a target for your tipping point—when you want your new career or business income to be enough that you can quit your day job—and keep that goal front and center in your thoughts and plans. Often, having that date or tangible financial goal burning in your mind can motivate you to make sacrifices to get there faster: move in with your parents temporarily, sell your car, or find a roommate.

Anyone entering this exciting transition phase should do so without debt. Ideally, you'll have at least six months of basic living expenses saved up before you leave your current job, plus already have a small but dependable income stream from your new business or freelance work.

Embrace Risk

There's no way around it: Change, big change, is full of risk. There is risk involved in changing careers. There are opportunities to fail when you push yourself outside of your comfort zone and try something new and foreign to you. What if you fail at switching careers? Worse, what if you put in all this work and find out you don't really want to be a restaurateur/project manager/carpenter? Unfortunately, there is a chance that even with a lot of preparation and training, your small business will fail.

Take comfort, though—minimalism can help you mitigate risk by lowering your cost of living and also by helping you build a profitable business. Startup costs you once thought mandatory (like an impressive office in an expensive location) can initially be replaced with minimalism-friendly options like working from home and meeting in cafés or client offices. If your business isn't web-based, a simple and inexpensive website will suffice over an expensive custom-designed website. There is always risk in starting a new venture, but keeping your overhead low and focusing on making your product or service the best it can be will reduce that risk.

The upside to taking risks is dramatic: great rewards. If you can't stop thinking about that dream career or business, or if you go to bed at night with business plans running through your mind, you owe it to yourself to take the risk for the bigger reward of a job you're excited to go to every morning. Doing work that you love is not always an easy path, but it is a rewarding one.

Enjoy Work Life More

Whether you want to work less or more or start
simplification and minimalism can help you rea
The simplified life, the one where you actually c
often reveals your true ambitions and feelings abc
Something that used to be the definition of success
company or position—might reveal itself to be trans
the other hand, sometimes removing the clutter an
more time reveals new or old career and business a
Whichever work path you choose, be it a new direction
ing stronger roots at your current job, minimalism will h
flourish.

Money

> **"** He who is contented is rich. **"**

—Lao Tzu

One of the beautiful things about minimalism is that there are many ways to simplify your life, but none of them requires more money. In fact, minimalism will help you rethink your entire approach to money.

Take a moment to think about your financial life. Do you feel in control of your spending habits? Are you living well below your means, or do you always hit a cash crunch at the end of the month? Are you often asking yourself, where did all my money go? Take heart in knowing that these are common struggles for most people, even those with well-paying jobs.

You Already Earn Enough

The minimalist secret to money is just that: you already earn enough. You can be in control of your finances, have enough money to pay your bills, save for your future, and still have funds leftover for things that bring value into your life. And you won't need to get a second job or sustain yourself on Ramen noodles alone to get there.

Minimalist money strategies are simple and effective, and can help you save more, work less, and invest in things that bring real value to your life. Once you've spent a few hours clearing out your home and donating things that you worked and paid for but rarely or never used, it's easy to see that buying more isn't a path to happiness. When you've reflected on your day and realized the highlight was watching the sunrise as you walked the dog before work (not the overpriced lunch out with colleagues), it's easy to see all the great things in your life that are free. This shift from looking outward for material happiness to looking inward for true contentment comes from making small changes to reduce the clutter and busy-ness in your life. This change of pace sheds light on what truly matters to you and what is worthy of your time, energy, and savings.

In this next section, we'll look at ways to reframe how we use money for contentment and how you can live happily within your means using the minimalist approach to money. Keep an open mind about these methods and strategies as you streamline your life and home. Some of these ideas may initially seem radical or far-flung or just plain impossible in your current life.

However, a little further into your minimalist journey, when your home is free of clutter and you have more than enough time for all the people and activities you enjoy, you may want to revisit this section for ways to trim your spending and financial obligations. The lure and joy of being able to Do Less quickly becomes a motivator for slashing bills and reducing your cost of living.

Minimalist Money Mindset

We each have our own unique money mindsets based on how we were raised and our history with money. We may have grand aspirations for wealth, or concrete retirement plans, or we might put a high value on having so-called disposable income. It might seem that minimalism can't possibly fit into all of these competing ideas and goals, but it can. We can all use minimalism to complement and help us reach our financial goals.

The first step to a minimalist money mindset is simply opening your mind to reshaping how you meet your goals. You need to get comfortable with being a bit uncomfortable and blow up some of your assumptions about how you have to spend your money. Just as you gave yourself some new eyes to reimagine what your home would look like without all that stuff, you'll now reimagine what your finances would look like if you had fewer obligations and more room for those goals and dreams.

Needs vs. Wants

Look closely at what you spend your money on. What is a need and what is a want? Beyond shelter, food, basic clothing, and medicine, everything else is usually a want. Yes, a haircut, going to the movies, that expensive blender that you just had to have to make smoothies—all wants. Some days it may feel like you really *need* that bigger television, but it is still firmly in the want category, along with five-dollar lattes and all-inclusive vacations.

Reconsidering Needs

Minimalism takes this line of questioning one step further to re-examine whether your needs truly are needs. For example, is your home in the need or want category? Could you live in something smaller, in a less expensive area? Could you move closer to work and reduce your commute and vehicle costs? If you moved into something smaller closer to your job, could you:

- Save an hour of driving a day?

- Save $500 in rent or mortgage payments a month?

- Save another $200 in vehicle costs a month?

- Use the freed-up time to exercise, get more sleep, or take up a hobby that you've been missing?

- Finally take that course you've wanted to take for a few years, the one that could lead to a career transition?

- Pay off those pesky student loans in a few years instead of twenty?

- Meet your retirement savings goals or have the cash to take that long-dreamed-of vacation?

- Finally have some breathing room in your budget?

As you can see, even within your "need" to have a house, there is a lot of leeway to live well on less. Moving is a big commitment, but it can bring quick and dramatic change to those who are short on time and money.

Smaller Wants Are Still Wants

The smaller wants in your life are usually masquerading as needs—expensive cell phones, new cars, and weekly Saturday night babysitters for dinners with friends. Tally up what your wants amount to for a month. Count everything that you don't truly need, including home Internet service, the lawn mowing service, and the monthly grooming service for your dog. It can be astounding to see how the small extras—the upgrades, the things we often think of as being needs rather than wants—eat up your dollars.

> **There will still be room in your minimalist life for luxuries and comforts.**

Now, if you're frightened about letting it all go—if you're scared that minimalism will mean a hard bed, gruel for dinner, and no heat in the winter—relax. There will still be room in your minimalist life for luxuries and comforts. The difference is that you will be thoughtful about these luxuries and comforts and they'll align with your value spending (more on that next).

The big upside to this approach: you'll enjoy those small luxuries more because you conscientiously decided to keep them in your life. You'll also enjoy your small luxuries more when you have them less frequently. Takeout pizza tastes best when you haven't had it in a few months, and the ease of taking a taxi somewhere is so much more enjoyable when you make the effort to walk or take the bus daily. By buying everyday luxuries less frequently, you'll save money and make those small treats you once took for granted feel like large extravagances.

Value Spending

Beyond simple shelter and food, we spend our money on what we value—hence the term "value spending." For some, that value is living in a large home in the suburbs, for others it's a sleek condo in the city, and for others it might be somewhere in between the two. Whereas one person may value the best cell phone or driving a newer car, another may put value on her education with evening courses and weekend retreats. No person's choice is better than another's.

What Choices Do You Make?

The key to understanding the root of value spending is this: you have a choice with how you spend your money. Yes, each time you open your wallet, it's a choice. What you value in life should be what you spend money on. Do you make thoughtful, planned decisions, or do you buy first and think later?

That doesn't mean the choices are easy, though. The size and location of your home, the type of car you drive, and your cell phone plan—these are big decisions, and in most cases, the minimalist approach is not the popular one. Yet, you *can*:

- Choose to live in a smaller home

- Get rid of the second car

- Live without cable (or even a television)

- Do away with your expensive cell phone plan

- Stop coloring your hair

Making minimalist decisions can simplify your life and free up money that you could put toward things you value more:

saving, travel, education, fitness, charity, and most of all, more time. Consider that by choosing the more expensive option in each of these cases, you're also choosing to:

- Work more

- Not have money for other things you want to do

- Add stress to your life by having lots of bills hanging over your head

Minimalist value-spending choices can be a challenge for many newcomers to the lifestyle. Take it slow, and start by prioritizing what you value in your life.

Personalized Value Spending

What do you value? List the top three things. It could be family, work success, your health, friendship, or creativity. How does your spending align with those values?

- If you value family and friendships, how do you spend your money so that you invest in those people and your relationship with them? Do you travel to see family and friends that are far away? Do you host large gatherings at your home?

- If health is something you value, do you spend your money on a personal trainer and organic food?

- If work success is at the top of your list, do you spend your money on household services so that you can spend more time working? Do you invest in career-specific education?

If you're not sure how much of your money is going to each category, make a quick tally of what you spend each month and what percentage of that spending is on the things you value most.

As you reflect on how your spending aligns with what you value, you may find that your values are nowhere to be seen. For example:

- You might value your community, but a large portion of your income is spent commuting into the city.

- You may say you value health, but your discretionary income is eaten up by takeout meals and your twice-daily latte habit.

This is not a time to feel regret or guilt. The conflict and misalignment between what you want and what you actually do is a challenge many people today face. Often you let yourself be pushed into spending money on things that your peers value or that you think you should value, instead of what truly speaks to you and your own wants and needs. This is, sadly, not that unusual. As you just saw when you uncluttered each room of your house in the Home section, it's very easy to buy, or in this case buy into, things you never needed or really wanted.

The exciting news is that you don't have to continue spending your money on things you don't really want. In these next sections, you'll create a plan to change your spending so you can Do Less and Live More.

Forget about the Joneses

One of the reasons our spending becomes so out of line with our values is that we think we need and want what those around us have. We should want a bigger home, a renovated kitchen, and an SUV that guzzles gas. We should be eating at restaurants as much as our friends do. We should be wearing the latest trends and fashions all the time. We should want and have everything we see our peers buying and doing.

The truth is, having everything has never made anyone happy. But if you've fallen into that trap, you're not alone. Many of us have sought out a promotion or new car, a new neighborhood, or even an elaborate wedding, with the idea that this one thing, a life milestone or massive purchase, will make us happy. But did it? The expense and stress involved with a wedding often brings unhappiness. The real contentment from a marriage doesn't come from a lavish wedding dress or an open bar, but from small moments and work that you put in daily over many years. If you're not happy with your life before you spend a lot of money on your dream kitchen with the subway tiles and granite countertops, you probably won't be happy after.

It sounds cliché, but spending money and buying things doesn't bring happiness. But having what you want—what you truly need for wellness and the time and focus to do things that really matter to you—that is a recipe for a contented life. Dismiss the idea that the conventional benchmarks of success—big house, new car, lavish vacations—are markers of happiness. In the minimalist life, you can make your own benchmarks for success, and they can be anything from sleeping in until noon every Saturday because you no longer have a lawn to mow to taking a month of unpaid leave from your job so that you can volunteer overseas. The possibilities for finding what truly brings contentment to your life are unlimited.

> **In the minimalist life, you can make your own benchmarks for success.**

When you let go of keeping up with the Joneses, you'll find the resources to actually have the things *you* really want. The minimalist life means charting your own path to happiness. It's a path that dismisses the frequent affordable luxuries so many of us think are necessities for bigger luxuries like time and financial freedom. As you pare down possessions and commitments to achieve these big luxuries, you'll start to see that the Joneses don't have it all. The Joneses have trapped themselves in a cycle of wanting more and spending more and none of it will ever be enough. More monthly payments will eat up the raise, and the bonus will go to keeping creditors at bay. In comparison, your raise or bonus or small windfall will be found money that you can spend or not spend as you please. That is the kind of flexible and easy freedom that comes from a minimalist life.

An easy way to forget about the Joneses? Stop comparing. Accept that all of us have different needs and wants. Yours won't be the same as your friends' and that's okay. The goal is not to live like everyone else but to know what brings value and joy to your life. Have the courage to fill your life with those people, hobbies, and activities, instead of the things those around you choose.

The Benefits of Delayed Gratification

It's all too easy to buy things today. Cheap clothing, everyday luxuries bought at the cosmetics counter, and inexpensive housewares at dollar stores make it easy to fritter away your money. All this cheap and easy stuff has made delayed gratification obsolete. Why bother waiting patiently and saving to buy that well-made wool coat that will last a decade when today you can buy the cheap synthetic knockoff that will last one season? We've lost the art of delayed gratification and our lives and homes are the worse for it.

Delayed gratification makes you value what you have more. Those impulse purchases are more likely to be lost or carelessly broken because you didn't work hard for them in the first place. But that new laptop that you saved for a year before buying? That laptop is treated with kid gloves and routinely cleaned and serviced so that it will last a long, long time. Not only do we treat the things we work hard for better, but we also enjoy them more. Dessert on a day when you played tennis for two hours is more satisfying than stuffing your face with chocolate at the movies when you haven't worked out all week. You value and enjoy what you work hard for, more than what you carelessly buy and consume.

Waiting for something makes you savor it more. When you wait all week to finally watch the season finale of your favorite television show, you enjoy it more than watching it while multitasking through household chores you can't put off. This works for the small and the big. Make a game of it. Challenge yourself to pack your lunch all week and put the money you save into an account marked for something special. When you finally hit your savings goal, you'll get more value from the purchase than what it actually cost. The work you put into waiting and building anticipation for the end result actually increases the enjoyment and value of it.

Practice Abundance

What if there was infinite money in your bank account? What if you never had to worry about a bill or mortgage payment or baseball fees or what that new furnace is going to cost? One trick to changing your mindset about money is to practice abundance. It sounds counterintuitive, but it doesn't mean spending every penny you have or pretending your annual salary has doubled. Instead, practicing abundance means freeing yourself of worries of scarcity. Here are three ways to practice abundance:

1. Give your time freely. If someone you know needs help, offer assistance without any worry about it negatively impacting your own needs or commitments.

2. Share your possessions freely. Give your stash of baby gear that you are saving for a potential future child away to people who can use it today. Loan your second car to a friend who can't afford to get hers fixed.

3. Don't worry about future needs. This doesn't mean not preparing for retirement or not planning who's going to pick the kids up from swimming tomorrow. It means that those problems you imagine in the future—the ones that could or could not happen, like losing your great job or urgent and expensive home repairs—shouldn't weigh heavily in your thoughts today. Do your best with the information at hand and the things that have actually happened or are on this week's calendar. If that "what if" scenario does happen, you can deal with it then. Don't bother worrying about it now.

When you practice abundance, you not only create more calm and less stress in your life, but you also practice the law of attraction. If you want good things to happen in your life, start by doing good things for others. If you think and act as if there is an abundance in this world, there will be.

Simple Money Tools

Being in control of your finances and spending doesn't need to be overly complicated or time-consuming. The goal with minimalism is to have to Do Less, not more. Complicated money-management systems often create more work and stress. The intention with minimalist money tools is to give you a clear picture of your spending and help you achieve your goals. Those goals could be spending less on transportation and more on health or reducing your monthly fixed costs so you can work less. You make the goals and then use these tools to help achieve them.

Budgets Are for Everyone

Budgeting can be fun. Really, it can. Whether you're a big earner or make an average wage, budgeting will allow you more freedom with your finances and help you meet your goals. It doesn't have to be complicated or boring. A lot of people feel budgets are meant to limit spending and that budgeting is really just another word for deprivation and saying no a lot. On the contrary, budgets can actually help you say yes more and also help you see that you are richer than you think.

So let go of your preconceived notions about budgets and also let go of any failed budgeting attempts you've made in the past. This time will be different. This time, you'll start with the minimalist approach: You already have all, and more, than you need.

Simplify Your Bills

Now that you've let go of keeping up with the Joneses and made note of how you spend money on your needs and wants, it's time to go minimalist with your bills. This is where the fun starts and where you start creating room in your budget for things like working less, saving more, and spending on things that actually bring value into your life.

The goal with a minimalist approach to finances is simplicity and awareness. You want to have a good understanding of where your money is going and not feel burdened by dozens of bills that are hard to keep track of and that hinder your cash flow. Ideally, you want to pay bills automatically each month, so you merely need to check your accounts online periodically to see that everything is running smoothly. If you find it hard to track what's coming in and what's going out of your bank account each month, or if you are overwhelmed by the sheer number of bills, it's a sign that your finances need a facelift. Re-evaluate everything beyond rent, utilities, and basic transportation.

Start by making a quick list of discretionary and nondiscretionary bills. Nondiscretionary bills are things like mortgage or rent, and home, life, and health insurance. As you tally your discretionary bills, make a note of which bills could be renegotiated or possibly reduced. Could you renegotiate your mortgage and knock $50 a month off of it? What about your life insurance or home insurance? Call the agents and review what your policy covers, if it's still appropriate for your life situation, and if they can offer you a better rate. Often one phone call can result in a few hundred dollars of savings each year.

Look at your nondiscretionary bills with an open mind. What are you really and truly using on a daily basis? Everything should be on the table for elimination or reduction. Do you really need the most comprehensive cell phone package? Do you read the newspaper daily or does it just fill up the recycling bin? If you do read the paper, could you read one at the office for free on your lunch break and switch to just receiving the weekend paper? If you have an expensive cable television package and a digital video recorder, think about how often you use them. Could a Netflix subscription and streaming television shows online save you $100 a month? Be open to experimenting with cutting services. Get over the fear that these changes have to be permanent. They don't. If you cut your cable package and then decide a few months later that you want it back, the provider will often offer you an incentive rate to get you to sign up again. Experiment with downsizing in different areas to find the extras and services that are easiest for you to part with.

> **Get over the fear that these changes have to be permanent. They don't.**

Dealing with Interest

If you're in debt, one of the most disheartening and challenging results from this exercise will be seeing how much you are paying each month in interest or mortgage points. You'll find more debt-reduction strategies in the rest of this book, but for now, look at ways to reduce your discretionary bills so you can put that extra money into your loans or credit card balances. Even a few small cuts to your "want" bills can free up money that will help accelerate debt repayment. For bigger wins on the debt-repayment front, look at larger expenses like rent and transportation and see if there is a way to live somewhere smaller and closer to work. Housing and transportation costs are two expenses we often think of as being fixed costs, and we often miss out on hundreds of dollars a month in savings because of that. Consider some short-term options like moving in with friends or selling your car and commuting by bike to makes big gains on paying off debt.

Reverse Budgeting

Reverse budgeting is so simple that there's no excuse not to try it. Here's the gist: When income comes in, set aside an amount for savings, perhaps having an automatic transfer of 10 percent of your income into another account, and the rest is yours to live off of until the next paycheck. That's it. When nondiscretionary bills like rent or your mortgage or medical insurance premium have been paid, the remaining money is yours to spend as you see fit. No categories, no tracking, and no complicated formula.

The beauty of this system is that it is simple and allows for flexibility. If you know you have a large expense coming up later in the month, live simply for a few weeks, inviting friends over for a movie night rather than joining them for a meal out. Delay any other large purchases. As you get closer to your next paycheck arriving, monitor your spending more frequently. Some weeks you may need to rustle up a few dinners from the staples in your pantry and freezer and other weeks you may have your paycheck come in with room to spare in your account. The goal is to learn how to say no when you need to and to keep an eye on your checking account balance. Some months you might have to pass on an event because you need new sneakers, but instead of feeling deprived, you feel at peace. You're living within your means and you now know that you don't need everything to be happy. And that knowledge is worth more than money.

Cash Is King

Paying with cash is the other cornerstone of a minimalist and easy budget system. Credit cards are often the gateway to overspending and mismanaging finances. Paying with cash is powerful and it's the easiest way to know what's left in your checking account. When you buy something with cash, you are instantly more aware of not only how much it will impact your bank balance but if the purchase is truly worth it. If you only have $400 left until payday and your cell phone bill still has to be paid, do you really have the cash to go on a road trip for the weekend? Credit cards allow you to conveniently forget the impact that buying something has on your bottom line. Using cash and cash only is an easy introduction to simple budgeting.

In a minimalist life, you use just what you have. Cash is what you have. Credit belongs to someone else: the bank.

Using a credit card complicates finances and can lead to spending more than you intend to. Parting with $70 in cash at the gas station can be a good reminder to batch your errands and drive less. It can even be motivation to ride-share, walk more, and consider moving closer to work. But handing over a piece of plastic at the pump doesn't have that same impact. It's too easy to forget that you put a purchase on a credit card and suddenly that healthy balance in your checking account is actually in the negative.

Sample Reverse Budget

Here is a simple spending plan for someone wanting to use a reverse budget.

- Monthly income after tax: $3,000

- Savings: $300

- Remaining money for all expenses: $2,700

Breakdown of expenses:

- Rent or mortgage: $900

- Utilities, cell phone, cable television, etc.: $300

- Transportation (car insurance, gas, repair, public transportation): $300

- Groceries and dining out: $600

- Other (charity, clothing, travel, home repair, etc.): $600

Reverse budgeting allows you greater flexibility than a budget that relies on categories or envelopes; it is also the simplest way to manage your money. When it's gone, it's gone, and when you have something left, you can choose where you'd like that money to go. Roll it over into next month's budget or send it to your savings account—it's your choice.

Get Out of Debt and Save More Money

If you're in debt, there is no better time than today, this very second, to start getting out of it. This book is full of ways to live simply and save money—use as many of them as you can. If you are in debt and it's holding you back from doing things you want, such as continuing your education, saving, or being able to work less, you have extra motivation to embrace these techniques. This section offers some practical and some radical ideas for getting out of debt and saving money.

Wait Thirty Days to Buy Something

One way to reduce your spending and avoid adding more debt and clutter is to wait thirty days before buying something. If you think you need a serving platter or a new swimsuit, promise yourself you'll buy it in thirty days if you think you still need it. Often, waiting on a purchase and living without it makes you realize either you already had something that did the job or you didn't really need the thing in the first place. We rarely get to hit the pause button in life, to take some time to think over our actions before we make them, and so we sometimes need to create these pauses artificially. That's what the thirty-day wait is: a pause to collect your thoughts instead of buying on impulse or without good intentions.

> **Often, waiting on a purchase and living without it makes you realize either you already had something that did the job or you didn't really need the thing in the first place.**

Waiting thirty days to purchase something is also a great way to practice delayed gratification. Everything in life is so instant now; no one has to wait for information or entertainment. If a shop is out of your size jeans, you can simply order them online with next-day delivery. Waiting is challenging for a lot of us because we aren't used to it. We can buy almost anything with a few clicks and a credit card today. As you turn your focus away from buying and consuming, you'll find it easier to wait for things and see that you need less than you once thought you did.

To put this into action, create a thirty-day buy list. You can use a notebook, a chalkboard, a list on your computer or smartphone, or a virtual pin board on something like Pinterest.com. When you think you need to buy something—anything that's not consumable or an emergency—put it on your list. Set a reminder on a calendar to check your list in thirty days. If, after thirty days, you still want the item and know it will be useful for you and fits in your budget, buy it. If, however, you realize you've been living well without that article of clothing/gadget/throw pillow, strike it from the list.

Shop with a List

Stores are organized and arranged to make us buy more than we intend to. The end-of-the-aisle display features a "loss leader" item, something the store is selling at a drastically reduced priced to get you to buy even more. A great deal is hard to resist! You may have come in to pick up just one item, but you end up leaving with a dozen. Stores can be a trap and undo the best intentions for sticking to a budget and just buying what you need.

In the Home section, you carefully went through each room and removed anything you weren't using or no longer needed. Think back to all those items you donated or sold. Did you buy them intentionally or were they purchased on a whim? Were you in a store looking for a gift for someone else when you decided to buy a little something for yourself too? Often the clutter we accumulate comes not from our planned purchases but from the unplanned ones. It's that stop at a craft store when you're killing time before meeting a friend for lunch or going to an electronics store to get a new battery for your laptop and leaving with a few DVDs and a universal overseas charger and adaptor too. Clutter and the unplanned purchase go hand in hand.

One strategy for sticking to a budget and buying just what you need: shop with a list. It's a simple way to keep focused while shopping and turn a blind eye to sale items or attractively displayed merchandise. Make a habit of only entering a store with a list in hand and your sale blinders on. Do not let the panic or fear that you are missing out on a good deal sway you into buying more than you intended. Sales come again, things can be bought secondhand for a better price, and losing out on one deal that could save you $5 is not worth layers and layers of clutter in your home and hundreds or thousands of dollars in wasted money. The good habit of shopping with a list will save you far more than any sale ever will.

To put this technique into action, consider where you write your shopping list. The back of an opened envelope, your day planner, or a note on your smartphone are all good spots for lists that will help you stay organized and focused. Pick the one that is easiest and make a habit of shopping with a list. Don't be concerned if you start off writing your grocery list sitting in your car parked outside the grocery store. It is always worth it to take a few minutes before entering a store to collect your thoughts and plan your shopping.

> **Clutter and the unplanned purchase go hand in hand.**

Stay Out of Stores

Even better than writing a list before you enter a store: don't go in the store. There are times when we need to browse to find an item—to see what is available and make a choice—but often, we go into a store for no other purpose than to see what they have without any idea of what we actually need. We're shopping not to find something we know we need, but to actually find the need. The idea of upgrading your cell phone or buying a soap dispenser didn't cross your mind until you saw the item in a store you were browsing. Suddenly that thing you didn't even know existed becomes something you must have.

The solution to all this false need is avoiding stores. This goes for brick-and-mortar stores and online shopping. If you don't have something on a list, preferably a consumable or something you've waited thirty days to buy, don't enter a store. Not going into a store is one of the easiest actions you can take to reduce clutter and save money. It's also a great way to save your time for more worthwhile pursuits such as sleep, making a good meal, or finding a spare hour to spend on yourself.

If shopping is a pastime for you or your friends, staying out of the stores will be a challenge. Start with finding other ways, preferably free, to socialize and bond. Instead of walking the mall, take a walk on a nature trail. Find new hobbies that don't center on buying things. Shopping shouldn't be a hobby! Hobbies should challenge you, like running, or relax you, like knitting. Your life will be richer, your bank account healthier, and your home less cluttered and easier to maintain when you stop shopping as a hobby.

Have a No-Spend Day

Sometimes it feels like all we ever do is open our wallets. Lunch, coffee, gas, $10 for a colleague's baby shower gift, and even feeding a parking meter all mean you're buying something. Wouldn't it be nice to spend a day without using your wallet at all? That's just what a no-spend day is. One day a week, decide you won't buy anything. Take your lunch to work and have your day planned out so that you could theoretically leave your wallet at home. Plan your shopping for an alternate day and book any social engagements or entertainment for a different night. If you have a daily purchase that you usually make with cash, such as bus fare, purchase a ticket the day prior.

The goal of a no-spend day is to get in the habit of living without spending. Too often, we think we need to spend money to have fun or to socialize. Our days are peppered with things that cost money but truly aren't necessities. The no-spend day gives you a fresh perspective on how to live with less stuff and on less money. When you're not constantly reaching for your wallet, you learn how to:

- Enjoy other aspects of your day . . . like the natural beauty that surrounds you as you walk home from work or listening to your favorite music as you fold laundry in the evening

- Sharpen your budgeting skills

- Heighten your senses for the free fun and joy in your life

It's a good way to spend less and learn how to enjoy your life more.

Unless you're living in a remote area with no Internet access, the chance to spend every day is almost unlimited. A morning coffee, an online order for running gear, lunch at the local sandwich shop, library fines, a half dozen items at the corner store when you just went in for milk, and a new mixing bowl set after you saw a sale sign in a kitchen shop window could be a normal day's purchases for most people. We open our wallets far too often and at the slightest provocation.

The minimalist life is one of financial simplicity, and part of that simplicity lies in spending with intention. For example: maybe you shop once a week because that is what works for your lifestyle. You make a point of not going to the grocery store in between those planned trips. At the end of the week, you might be having your coffee black and your breakfast is last night's leftovers on a piece of toast, but that isn't a hardship. You are simply using things up, limiting waste, and sticking to a once-a-week shopping routine that saves you time and money. That's just one way to spend with intention. Another way is to leave your wallet at home when you don't plan on buying anything. Having to go home and get your wallet quenches the need to buy something.

> **The minimalist life is one of financial simplicity, and part of that simplicity lies in spending with intention.**

Be intentional about when and how you spend money. Remind yourself that you have a choice. Making this small habit of not spending one day of the week will help you be more mindful of all the other times you open your wallet.

Get Out of Debt

Debt complicates your life. Debt makes your life more challenging and it prevents you from doing the things you want to do: changing careers, working less, or taking that dream vacation. If you have any debts beyond a mortgage, work quickly and methodically to pay them off. Debt holds you back, and the goal of adopting a more minimalist life is to move forward.

First, let go of your guilt about bad financial decisions and money you've wasted in the past. If you followed the guide to decluttering your home in the earlier section of this book, you probably got rid of a lot of things that you paid good money for. You may have even donated things that you are still paying for or sold them for a fraction of the original price. When you have a moment of sadness or guilt about your financial past, remember this: The money is already gone. The one positive thing you can do now is to start spending and saving wisely.

Find What's Easy to Do Without

One trick to getting out of debt without being miserable is to know what your rice and beans are. This means, if you can live off repetitive and inexpensive meals and it won't make you greatly unhappy, do it. If, however, you know that cutting your grocery budget will make you miserable, that a ham sandwich and an apple for lunch seven days a week might make you lose your will to live, find another area of your life that you can painlessly trim. That may mean walking to work instead of taking the bus or switching to a no-data cell phone or moving back in with your parents for a year. Find that cost-cutting measure that, though not easy, won't make you feel so deprived and unhappy that you'll start increasing your spending in other areas to compensate.

Keep a few small luxuries. It could be your Friday lunch out with coworkers or your yoga classes. Actually call them luxuries so that you remember they aren't necessities. Keep them on a list in your wallet and look at them when you're feeling like you want to spend money.

Stay Motivated Through Tough Times

Be bold in your debt-reduction plans. This could mean moving, selling your car, or getting an extra job for a little while. Some short-term discomfort is well worth the long-term freedom of being debt-free. You can also take a look at your discretionary and nondiscretionary bills again and review what you can really live without. Don't think too far ahead on some of your get-out-of-debt plans. It's true, you might want to rejoin that gym at some point or have a landline phone again, but right now, saving that extra money each month to pay down your debt is worth it.

Find a confidant to keep you honest and motivated when it gets tough. This could be a friend, a sibling, your spouse, or even virtual friends. Join an online forum for personal finance or start a blog to track and write about your debt-reduction plans. Paying off debt is a marathon, not a sprint, and it helps to have a support network when you feel your resolve slipping or you need more ideas for cutting costs.

Remember What's Free

Sometimes it is hard to see all the fun that can be had without spending a dime. As you scale back your spending, make a list of the no-cost fun in your life. Books from the library, hosting a potluck dinner, pick-up basketball at the local courts, and a long bath are all mostly free activities. Keep adding to your list as you remember more things that you enjoy that don't require money. When you're tempted to hit the movies for the latest blockbuster and jumbo popcorn, ask a friend over for a movie night. If your friends are all spenders and in a habit of buying expensive concert tickets or do a lot of casual dining out, try to gently steer them into more wallet-friendly fun.

Rethink Home Ownership

Here's a statistic that will shock you: Renters are actually happier than homeowners. A study published in 2009 from the University of Pennsylvania's Wharton School showed that homeowners are no happier than renters in life satisfaction, overall mood, and overall feeling and actually derive more pain from their homes. Another interesting comparison between homeowners and renters: the owners were on average twelve pounds heavier than the renters. Perhaps this increase in weight is because owners also had less active leisure time than the renters. So renting could actually be better for your health.

Friends and the bank may try to convince you owning a home is a necessity, but it certainly isn't a requirement for a happy life. The dream of home ownership isn't all it's cracked up to be. The renter simply makes a call when the stove breaks or the sink backs up; the homeowner deals with the stress and cost of repairs. Many of us stretch our finances as far as the bank allows so we can buy a home. The burden of a large mortgage, constant repairs, and nonstop responsibility affects your quality of life. Owning a home might not be the right path for you if you want flexibility in your work, if you want to change careers, if you work in a fulfilling but not well-paying job, or if you simply want weekends free to go rock climbing. Not everyone needs to own a home.

Buy Secondhand

A minimalist approach means not only buying less but spending less too. A great way to spend less is to buy secondhand. There are a few things you would never purchase secondhand, of course, but most things in a home can be easily sourced lightly used for a fraction of what they originally cost. Secondhand is for the savvy shopper, the wannabe minimalist, the environmentally conscious, anyone getting out of debt, and anyone who wants to save his money for things that bring more value into his life.

If you're new to buying secondhand, start slowly, getting to know where you can buy good-condition preowned clothing and goods for a fraction of their retail price. eBay.com is a wonderful resource for buying secondhand and allows you to quickly and efficiently search for exactly what you need. Get familiar with local buy-and-sell websites and boards. Thrift stores are also great for secondhand items but require an eye for value, patience, and focus. Plus, it's easy to get distracted by all the interesting junk in thrift stores and forget about what you originally came in to look for! If you've struggled to rein in your casual shopping habits, thrift stores may not be for you.

It takes more time to buy secondhand and you'll need to be patient if there is something you specifically need. Instead of hitting refresh on the local buy-and-sell online forum, make an appointment with yourself to just check once a week for that desk/lamp/bike. Just like your Thirty-Day Buy List, this barrier to spending can actually help you see that you either don't need the item or could get by with something smaller or less expensive.

How to Be Rich Without a Lot of Money

Yes, you can be rich without a lot of money. Sure, we all need some income, but there are riches to be had beyond your stock portfolio. A key tenet to minimalism is to maximize what you do have for the greatest effect. If you have your health, great friends, and burning creative aspirations, use them as your barometer of wealth instead of money.

Every great evening laughing with your closest friends is money in the coffers of a rich life. Every leisurely walk you take with your dog or a friend or on your own, enjoying nature, shows you your wealth of time and health. Every hour spent on work you find value in, be it a creative outlet like sewing, a fulfilling hobby like auto repair, or your job, fills the coffers of a life well lived. You can feel wealthy no matter what your income bracket is.

> **A key tenet to minimalism is to maximize what you do have for the greatest effect.**

Life

> **"** The secret of happiness, you see, is not found in seeking more, but in developing the capacity to enjoy less. **"**

—Socrates

It has never been easier to stay in touch with friends and family, make social plans, and pursue a wide variety of sports, activities, and hobbies, sometimes at any hour of the day. We have so much competing for our attention, money, and time. There are no limits to the hours you can spend updating your online status, researching anything and everything on the

Internet, and checking your e-mail multiple times an hour. The once-a-month book-club dinner, the school council meeting, and the recreational volleyball team fill up nights. All the chores required to maintain your home take up the remaining hours of the week. There are so many ways to spend our time we're often overwhelmed with too many options vying for our nonwork hours. Too many choices leave us in a perpetual state of busy.

What Do You Really Want to Do?

We're so busy that the causes, people, and activities we really love, the ones that we find most rewarding, often get the least amount of our time. We're so busy running from one thing to the next, saying yes to every invitation, every request for our precious time, reading every update from every acquaintance, that we don't have the focus or wherewithal to use our time wisely and with intention.

The minimalist approach to life outside of work frees up your time and energy so you can spend it on things that really matter to you. As you apply the minimalist concept to household chores, your television and Internet habits, and even your friends, you will not only create more time but get more enjoyment from those things you hold most dear. As you discovered in the Money section, removing the clutter in your schedule and obligations will more closely align your time with your values.

Count the hours in your day and consider what you did with them. Be as detailed as you can. If you zoned out in front of the television for three hours, half-watching a few television shows and half-surfing the Internet, include that description in your hour count. Try to remember the ten minutes standing in line at the coffee shop and the thirty minutes you spent on what was supposed to be a quick grocery shop. Now, go through and determine what was leisure and what was work. Include household chores and driving in the work category. If you look at the hours, does your list align with how you think you spend your time? Does it align with your values? Do you value time with your spouse, but between your commute, making dinner, last-minute evening errands, and television, you only make time for fifteen minutes of distracted conversation each day? Your time is too valuable to give away that carelessly.

Take back those hours that you're losing to things that don't align with your values. Minimalism offers many ideas for big and small ways to get more time:

- Declutter your home so it's easier to clean and to find things.

- Shop less, not only to take back those hours lost to the mall or grocery store, but also to reduce your income needs.

- Limit social media and your phone interruptions so you can get those big and small things done and enjoy your sleep and leisure time to the fullest.

- Think about bigger changes, like moving closer to work to reduce a commute or moving into a smaller home so that you can work part-time.

- Try out a few minimalist lifestyle changes, like cutting cable television or only using the Internet once in the morning, and see if they give you more time for those things you want more of.

When an opportunity arises that requires your time, determine if it fits into your values before committing to it. It is so easy to get swept up by the tide of other peoples' desires and wants when it's not truly a cause or activity that feeds your soul and fits into your own plan. You really can't do everything, so you must be discerning about whom and what you give your time to.

Time is finite. We only have so many hours in our days, really in our lives, to spend. It can be easy to think each moment doesn't count, that a weekend lost to cleaning out the garage for the second time that year isn't a big deal, but it all adds up. Soon the trivial and the self-inflicted work take all your time, and it's not only challenging to find the hours for your own passions—it's hard to even remember what they are! If you say yes to everything, you'll end up saying no to things you actually want.

Habits

A key to keeping that clutter in your home and life gone for good: habits. Good habits make for an easy life. Good habits make hard things effortless:

- Your daily run becomes automatic when it's a habit.

- The counters and sink are clear when you put your dirty dishes in the dishwasher directly after meals instead of letting them sit.

- When you always go to bed before eleven o'clock, you don't need to hit snooze on your alarm and you always catch the early bus for work.

If you want to use minimalism for an organized, happy, and uncluttered life, it's important to have a few cornerstone habits to keep you on track.

Single-Tasking

One skill you need to master to take advantage of a minimalist lifestyle: single-tasking. Our world is focused on the opposite—doing many things at once. We take phone calls while on the treadmill and have text-message conversations during movies. Focusing on one thing at a time allows you to engage deeply in your interactions. It helps you finish an unpleasant chore faster and gives you more value for your ticket price at a movie or event. Single-tasking also helps you manage your time more efficiently by allowing you to easily see what is most important to you.

You don't need to get more things done faster; you need to do fewer things better. Multitasking is overrated. Sure, a bit of music playing in the background while you complete some repetitive chores is fine, but cooking dinner while you're having a conversation by Instant Messenger and watching a television show and keeping an eye on the sick dog—it's too much for anyone. Multitasking leads to errors, big and small. You might multitask and end up burning dinner, or even worse, get in a car accident. You also miss the small beautiful moments when you multitask. The great conversation is interrupted by a phone call from the drycleaner and the spectacle of a gorgeous sunrise is lost to taking a photo of it so you can share it online.

> **You don't need to get more things done faster; you need to do fewer things better.**

The Benefit of Routines

Routines are an integral part of an exciting and fruitful life. Surprised to read that? Routines get a bad rap for their association with boredom or monotony, when in fact they can be a gateway to productivity and make room for spontaneity and excitement. The important step is to identify what areas of life are ideal for routine and what areas are best kept free for last-minute decisions. This gives you more room for choice where you need it and when you want it. Ask yourself where you like choice and where you like routine:

- Do you need variety in your breakfast or are you a creature of habit and eat a bowl of cereal six of seven mornings a week?

- Would you be comfortable wearing the same outfit every Monday to work or do you like deciding what to wear every morning?

To get the benefit of routines, first look for the ones you already have and which ones you enjoy most. The goal is to batch small decisions into routines so you don't have to put any energy or time into making choices.

Routines simplify our lives. Taking the same route to work, catching the same bus every morning, sweating through the same spin class every Tuesday night—all those things make our lives easier and leave more energy for the bigger goals and dreams we have. Consider:

- If you eat salmon every Tuesday night, you don't have to waste time that afternoon thinking about or planning a meal.

- If you always go for a run first thing Saturday morning, you don't hesitate or debate putting your running shoes on and getting out the door.

- If you wake up at the same time every weekday morning, and conversely go to bed within the same half-hour window Sunday through Thursday, you don't have to debate if you should stay up an extra hour to finish that book or watch more television or surf the Internet.

Routines declutter your daily schedule and give you more time. When you're looking for ways to get more of what you want, be it time for work, rest, or play, one thing that can help is having set morning and evening routines. When you wake, you're on autopilot for your first hour preparing for the day ahead and you arrive at your desk awake, on time, and ready for an efficient and productive morning at work.

Make note of the routines you keep. Does every day start and end at a different time? Do you awake and instantly start asking yourself, what next? Are there dozens of decisions to make before you put your coat on and go outside? Do you spend Sunday night wondering how you'll make the time to pay bills or do housework in the following week? Remove these questions from your life by building routines for them.

Building Your Own Routines

There are many things you can turn into a set routine to free up your time. Here is a list of tasks you can automate for yourself.

- **Meals:** Have the same breakfast all week at the same time. Set a dinner hour and stick to it.

- **Sleep:** Go to bed in the same one-hour window each evening. Enjoy half an hour of screen-free time before you hit the sheets. Set your alarm for the same time each morning.

- **Clothing:** Select five outfits, one for each weekday, and stick to the same Monday-to-Friday rotation.

- **Housework:** Set a weekly cleaning and laundry routine. Be specific about the tasks, the time of day you will perform them, and how long you will take.

- **Grocery shopping and meal preparation:** If you have a traditional Monday-to-Friday workweek, shop for groceries at the beginning or end of the week. Commit to just going to the grocery store once a week with a meal plan and list in hand so that you don't have to waste time, energy, and money on last-minute trips to the store for ingredients vital to the evening meal.

Get Rid of Junk Mail

Paper clutter is insidious. We all have it: the opened but not filed or shredded bills that sit on the kitchen counter for a week before you move them to the home office, where they languish for weeks; fliers and junk mail that need to be sorted, recycled, shredded, or filed. One way to reduce the work involved in staying on top of clutter is to limit what comes into the home. Get rid of as much junk mail as you possibly can. Here are some tips:

- Start by contacting your local post office and finding out how to get off their flier delivery service.

- Do you get thick stacks of seasonal catalogues? Contact the companies directly and get yourself removed from their mailing lists. Most, if not all, companies have websites you can browse if you prefer to shop from home. A few phone calls and e-mails can save you several hours a month of sorting paper clutter.

▧ Going "paperless" was supposed to be a milestone for the new millennium. Yet, we seem to have more paper to deal with and now more electronic statements flooding our e-mail than we did just a few years ago. Staying organized has never been harder. The solution: truly go paperless. Notify your bank and any company you receive a statement from that you only want to receive electronic statements. Some companies will allow you to make this switch on their website, whereas others will require that you call them. Be sure to request paperless statements for every bank account, investment account, and credit card. To avoid ending up with digital clutter from the online statements, create folders and categories within your e-mail account to save electronic statements. If the statement arrives as an attachment, create a folder on your computer to save all your statements. Remember to stick to the same naming scheme for all folders and subfolders, such as year, company, and account name.

Now that you have less coming into your home, you can finally tackle all that paper clutter in your home office. Check back in the Home section for more ideas for culling all the paper clutter in your home.

Take Fewer Photos

How many photos do you have of your infanthood? Most likely you have far fewer photos of yourself crawling, eating birthday cake, and enjoying your first beach vacation than the average child today. Digital photography has changed not only how we take photographs but also how many pictures we take. It's so easy to take photos that we take thousands of them a year instead of just a few dozen on special occasions. We take photos of our meals and send them to friends and post them on social media websites. We take multiple photos as we try to capture the perfect smile. Are all these photos worthy of framing and being displayed in our homes? No. Yet we keep all these digital files and they clog up our computers and cell phones, making it impossible to find the ones we need when we need them.

The two best ways to reduce all this electronic clutter: take fewer photos and delete everything but the best.

1. Wait for those really special moments before you pull out your camera. Not only will you capture better images, but you'll also see more and enjoy more when you're not constantly trying to document everything.

2. After you've taken photos, quickly delete from your camera any that you know aren't worth keeping. When you upload photos to your computer or a digital photo album, edit them again to include just the very best pictures.

If you can make these two things a habit, you will not only need less electronic storage for your photos, but you'll have better images that are easier to find when you need them. Plus, you'll enjoy life more when you're not always behind the camera trying to capture every single moment.

Meal Planning

It can seem counterintuitive, but to Do Less in the kitchen you first need to plan more. In the Home section, you reduced your kitchen clutter by just keeping cookware to make six of your favorite weekday meals. Those six meals plus a simple set of breakfast and lunch items will revolutionize how much time, money, and effort you put into cooking healthy and fresh meals. Fast, simple, and healthy beats messy, complicated, and expensive any day.

Meal planning is a cornerstone of a waste-free, frugal, and minimalist kitchen. By knowing what's for dinner in advance, and having all the ingredients on hand, you reduce your daily stress and free up more of your time. No more last-minute runs to the store, or even worse, losing all your cooking motivation and ordering take-out. You don't need an app or a binder or a complicated spreadsheet to meal plan, either. You just need six simple meals that you can throw together on weeknights.

If you've never meal planned before, don't be scared. Meal planning is just another way to live an organized and intentional life. It will help you eat nutritious meals, save money, and never face the four o'clock "what's for dinner?" panic again.

Start with your list of six simple meals. They should be meals that you can pull together in thirty minutes or less of final preparation and cooking time. Think grilled chicken thighs instead of a whole roasted chicken, or a stew that can be loaded into a slow cooker in the morning instead of cooked in a Dutch oven for three hours in the afternoon. Save complicated or time-consuming recipes for special occasions.

Meals Don't Have to Be Boring

To cut down on the number of ingredients, look for recipes that have a few items in common with each other. Ideally you have a few crossover items like grains or vegetables that you can buy and prepare in bulk. Don't be afraid to duplicate side dishes in a week. Variety may be the spice of life, but it tends to take up a lot of time and space in your refrigerator.

Create a list of your meals and all their ingredients. If your list is long and dotted with things like fresh basil, anchovy paste, and kumquats, go back to the drawing board. Simple can be just as interesting and tasty as complicated. Simple can be as sophisticated and gourmet as you want it to be. Here are some suggestions:

- Pan-fry salmon with a squeeze of lemon and add a side of broccoli and rice.

- Make a double batch of rice and turn it into fried rice the next night with chicken, whatever vegetables are in need of use, and a dash of soy sauce.

- A large batch of Bolognese sauce for spaghetti can be quickly turned into chili the following night with the addition of a can of beans and chili powder.

Hearty, simple meals are the foundation of minimalist meal planning. Save the experimenting for a weekend when you want to have fun and entertain.

Even the most organized and streamlined life is peppered with the occasional busy day followed by take-out or more leftovers than anticipated. For this reason, only plan for six evening meals a week.

Isn't That Boring?

Some people view meal planning as boring and think it removes some spontaneity from life. But in the organized and happy life, meal planning allows for spontaneity in bigger things:

- If you meal plan regularly, you reduce food waste and save money.

- If you meal plan regularly, you save time by not having to go to the grocery store more than once a week. Without the stress of last-minute dinner planning you can put your energy, time, and money into bigger goals.

- If you meal plan, you create more space in your life for things like last-minute weekend getaways, turning the evening meal into a picnic, and having the funds to enjoy a planned meal out with friends.

Of course, if cooking is a hobby that you value, you might find that you *want* to spend more time on it. If so, go ahead! The point of minimalism is to spend more time doing what you love. If that's cooking, then free up time and money using other ideas in this book and spend yours on cooking.

Go to Bed Early

How many mornings does your alarm go off and you regret that extra hour, or three, you stayed up the night before? With the exception of New Year's Eve or a big night on the town, it's rarely worth it to stay up past eleven o'clock if you have to be at work by nine the next morning. If you let yourself get consumed by a book, a craft project, the Internet, work, or bad television, you'll often feel exhausted the next day. There are endless ways to waste the late hours of the evening that will fill you with regret the next day. You might find yourself groggy, late, and short-tempered because you made a small but bad decision to stay up too late the night before.

Going to bed early simplifies your life because it makes your days easier. A good night's sleep brings more patience, energy, and focus for family and work. Make yourself an adult bedtime routine:

▧ Avoid stressful conversations or activities after 8:00 P.M.

▧ Turn computers, smartphones, tablets, and televisions off by 9:30 P.M.

- Spend a few minutes on self-care. Floss. Actually clean your contact lenses instead of just shoving them in their case. Do a nice wash and cleanse with those skin products that you splurged on but never make the time to use.

- Settle into bed thirty minutes before you hope to be asleep. If you're going to read in bed, set a page or time limit for yourself.

What time you go to bed each night has a big impact on your life. Go to bed at the same time each evening and reap the rewards of great sleep and a good start to each day.

Watch Less Television

Nowadays, there are many ways to watch your favorite television shows. You can watch through regular cable subscription, record the show to watch later, or stream it online. You don't need to kill time watching not-so-great television as you wait for your favorite program to air.

If you want more time for your favorite things—sleep or your spouse or reading or playing ball with your son—watch less television. Set a weekly limit for yourself, similar to what you might do for your children, and prioritize the programs you want to watch. If you're used to the television being on whenever you are home, start leaving it off and only turn it on when you are ready to enjoy a quality program that you have already selected. Resist the temptation to surf channels. Being a deliberate and discerning television viewer is one way to create more time in your schedule and reduce distractions.

Manage Internet Usage

Screen time is no longer limited to living rooms or movie theaters. We can watch a movie while sitting on a bus or play a video game while at a restaurant. With great Internet and media availability comes great temptation. Feeling bored or unmotivated at work? There are literally a billion things to watch or read on the Internet. Tempted to order a pizza at ten o'clock at night even though you should really go to bed? A few taps on your tablet computer and a deep-dish pepperoni is on its way.

The Internet and mobile online technology have brought us so much freedom and also so much wasted time. We've become so used to rapid-fire information, text messages flowing in, and online news headlines changing on the hour, that it's hard for us to actually focus on something or someone exclusively for longer than a few minutes. We've become so connected to our cell phones and computers that we can't relax when we're away from them. Many of us feel enslaved to all this new technology. This all-day connectedness is enough of a problem that people are now paying to go on vacations or retreats where there are no cell phones and anything that connects to the Internet is confiscated on arrival.

We don't have to let our days be driven by instant messages and hitting refresh on an Internet browser. Taking a step back from technology and being online is the first step in gaining more hours in your day. Start by honestly tracking how many times a day you check your e-mail or log into a social media site. See if you can reduce the frequency to just once or twice a day.

Align your time with your values and goals and push yourself to focus on just one task at a time, be it making a meal or folding laundry. Take the urgency and compulsion to just "check one more thing" away by putting your cell phone and laptop away and out of view when you want to focus on other things—especially people.

If you struggle with spending too much time online, if the need to be connected online hinders your ability to do things you value, start to slowly wean yourself from online activities and add in engaging no-screen-required hobbies. It may help to tell friends and family about your goals and make plans with them where you both commit to no cell phones or being online. Treat your Internet time as you would food if you were working on your nutrition or trying to lose weight. Set limits, monitor your consumption, and find alternate ways to keep yourself engaged and active.

> **Treat your Internet time as you would food if you were working on your nutrition or trying to lose weight.**

Hobbies and Activities

What's the goal of all this decluttering and reprioritizing of your life and work? More time for things you love. The end result is creating time, money, and space to do things that you truly enjoy and that are of value to you.

Hobbies vs. Social Pressure

Take a cursory glance at a current home décor or lifestyle magazine and you'll see that the number of craft or do-it-yourself projects is overwhelming. Where and how do people find the time to do all these sewing and woodworking projects? Don't they have jobs to go to? The world of blogging and sites likes Facebook.com and Pinterest.com just provide more fodder for the super-hobbyist who seems to need only three hours of sleep a night.

The pressure to do everything and have it all—the home-made sprouted grain bread, the bathroom painstakingly reno-vated with no help from professionals, and the rigorous amateur triathlon-training schedule—is abundant. It's also a pressure that brings layers of stress and loss with it: for every hand-made Halloween costume, there is a takeout pizza dinner and a mother with bags under her eyes. No one does it all—they just show us the best of themselves in the moments they are very proud of. Accept this, understand it, and move on so you can enjoy the things you are good at and stop trying to do it all.

Hobbies should be things we do to relieve stress, relax, and feel good. One way we confuse ourselves when we try to have it all is by thinking that hobbies are required. Making your own deodorant from scratch is a hobby, not a necessity. Even exercise, a requirement for a healthy life, has to be viewed as a hobby. Those things you give your time to beyond work, sleep, and eating have to be recognized as optional. If they're not, you'll never get past this idea that you can do it all. Trust me: You don't have to hunt down dinner in the woods or train for an open-water swimming competition to have a rewarding life.

What Are Your Hobbies?

With this in mind, think about your hobbies and write them down. Include every last one of them. Those half-finished home projects and the tennis rackets you haven't used in years should be somewhere on your hobby list. Anything beyond your basic kitchen equipment should be represented on the list: cake decorating, canning, fresh pasta–making. If you own a sewing machine, sewing must be one of your hobbies. If you have a workbench with tools, home repair is a hobby. Nothing is too big or too small to be on this list.

Also include on your hobby list any obligations outside of work: committees, teams, friends, fitness, and sports. If you regularly have yard work to do on weekends, meet once a week for coffee with your mother, or spend seven hours a week driving your children to and from school, put it all on the list. This is a chance to really see the people and activities you spend your time on.

Pick Three Hobbies

Now make a list of things that make you happy. Is one of your hobbies on that list? It should be. Your list might be as long as a dozen things. The truth? It's probably impossible for you to do them all. So pick three top choices and allow yourself the time, space, and money to enjoy them properly.

Simplifying means getting rid of what you don't enjoy so you can focus more on what you do enjoy. If that box of découpage supplies makes you feel guilty since you bought it on a whim and haven't made anything with it in the two years since, let it go. Someone else, probably someone you know, will be only too happy to take your unused goods.

Worried about the "what ifs" again? As in, what if you find the time or motivation to take up a sport or hobby and you've sold or given away all your equipment and supplies? Well, that would be a good problem to have. You could buy skis again secondhand when your schedule allows you to be a regular skier again.

Hobbies are meant to enrich your life and be special pastimes. They are not meant to be burdens that clutter your home and schedule. So keep just hobbies you enjoy regularly in your life and pass on the equipment or cancel your membership for the rest.

Quit Something

When was the last time you quit something? Not a diet or exercise routine, but a committee or club. If you are low on time and high on stress, consider quitting one of your obligations. Step down from your seat on the Parent Teacher Association, drop out of the Wednesday night language club that you dread every week, and even consider quitting a social media website. If you have children and are driving back and forth across the city to their music and sport practices, ask *them* to quit one, or two, or four of those lessons. Often we feel that we have to sign up for the lesson or the team when, in fact, everything is optional. You don't have to have a Facebook.com account, your child doesn't have to take gymnastics lessons, and you certainly don't have to be a part of every committee that asks you to be a member.

If it frightens you to quit or say no to something, start with a trial absence. Take a semester off, put your account on hold for a month, and tell your softball team you won't be available this season. Get a taste for what it feels like to not have every hour of your week blocked off with obligations. Find out how it tastes to eat leisurely weekday breakfasts, at the table and not in your car. This slice of the sweet and simple life, one without hours in the car and rushed meals, may convert you to the Do Less mantra.

> **If it frightens you to quit or say no to something, start with a trial absence.**

If you're concerned about your children not participating in multiple sports and clubs, determine what they are excelling at and have a genuine interest in and then reduce based on that list. Today's kids need more unstructured time for play and exploration, and yes, even for doing nothing much at all. Over-scheduling of school children, even preschoolers, is a modern problem and the result is stressed-out families and kids. Included in the stress are all the fees for classes and extra tuition that come along with these extracurricular activities. So save your kids' sanity, and your own, and place some much-needed breaks into your weekday schedule.

Try Something New

Do you look through the evening-class catalogue from the local college every semester but never sign up for anything? Do you diligently read all the offerings on the bulletin board at the coffee shop, wistfully looking at ads for sitar lessons and foreign language conversation clubs, but never take one of the little strips of paper with the contact information? Now that you've decluttered your life of hobbies that weren't priorities, try something new. Learning a new skill sharpens the mind and sparks creativity.

Put Away Your Cell Phone

Want to enjoy your hobbies and friends more? Want to savor the taste of that expensive steak or laugh out loud at that sitcom?

Start by putting your cell phone away. Most of us don't need to be available by phone at every hour of the day. And yet we are. We let phone calls and text messages interrupt the good and bad in our lives. When someone calls during a particularly wonderful or stressful moment we tend to blame our phones for interrupting us. Yet, we control our cell phones. We can turn them off or on and we can silence them.

Try it: Silence your phone. Silence it so you can engage with yourself, the person in front of you, and whatever work or activity you are giving your time to. If you turn your phone off or, even better, leave it at home, you can focus. It's not always easy, particularly when you're with people who give their cell phones a place at the table, but it is well worth it.

If you find the idea of not having your cell phone on or at hand stressful, start with small steps. Put your cell phone on silent for an afternoon and try to not check it for two to three hours. Slowly increase your cell phone–free time from there. Remember, it's okay to not answer your phone. You don't need to be available to everyone at every hour of the day. You can call people back when it suits you and you can let people know you were busy. Sleep, relaxing, and having time when you're really not doing much at all are adequate reasons to not be available by phone.

If you're concerned about what your new availability will do to existing friendships, simply let your friends in on the plan. Talk about your reasons for putting your phone away or not answering it and discuss this lifestyle change as if it were a new workout regime or a restructuring of your work hours. Also share how it benefits your friendship: You want to be more present and less distracted when you are spending time with them.

Relationships

Dunbar's number is a theory that we have a limit to the number of relationships we can have. British anthropologist Robin Dunbar developed this theory based on a correlation between primate brain sizes and average social group size. For the average human it means our brain size allows us to relate to and remember the relationships of about 150 people. After that we don't have the cognitive ability to remember each person and his relationship to us and to the other 149 people. This number is just for acquaintances and colleagues. This isn't a number for an inner circle of close friends and confidants. This is the sum of names you can remember and put to faces while also recalling that they volunteer at the library.

Consider Dunbar's number when you look at your social media connections. Sure, being friends on Facebook.com might help you remember someone's name, but at what cost? If the number of people whose names and relationships you can accurately remember is 150, how many people can you have deep and meaningful and reciprocal relationships with? How many people can you give your time to and know well enough to be able to ask for help and give help in a crisis? How many people can you allow into your life and still have space and energy for your own needs and dreams? How many people can you read updates from, take phone calls from, and spend time with face-to-face? For a lot of us, that number is just a fraction of Dunbar's number of 150.

Letting Go of Old Friendships

As you remove the unneeded from your life, as you declutter to get to the heart of what you want more of, as you remember the simple things that bring a lot of happiness into your life, sometimes you see that you have to declutter your friends, too. You might have to let go of a few people so you can make more room for deeper friendships and be a better friend to those closest to you. You might have to let go of people that you don't bring out the best in and that don't bring out the best in you.

Which friends do you let go of? Just as you wouldn't keep clothing from junior high school to wear or books from primary school to read, you can let go of friends that you have outgrown. Perhaps you have each taken different paths in life and they no longer converge or even run parallel. Despite no common interests and no deep-shared history or roots, you've kept up the mechanics of friendship. There may be a few indicators that you have both outgrown each other, but neither of you has come to terms with it enough to let go. It's time to let go if you feel:

- Dread when the person calls

- Guilt when you realize you haven't seen him in months

- Regret when you spend time with the person but are constantly checking your watch

View it as the ultimate act of kindness. You no longer need to waste each other's time.

Removing Negative Relationships from Your Life

You can also let go of negative relationships. As part of your minimalist approach to happiness, as part of your new edict to Do Less and do things well, you don't have room for people who speak negatively about you or to you. In the quest for a happy and organized life, you may have to walk away from some friendships in order to let others thrive. Even if the person has done negative things in the past, you've likely justified the friendship in one way or another, which can make it difficult to leave. How do you gently break away from a friend? Most likely the seed has already been planted. Remember, if you're not getting something positive out of the relationship, it's likely the other person isn't either.

The easiest way is not to return that next phone call or to decline an invitation to meet up by e-mail. After a few missed connections, the friendship will eventually peter out. If you want a swifter approach, muster some courage, remind yourself that this is for the good of both parties, and sit down with your friend for a candid conversation. The same rules that apply to breaking up a romance—empathy and discretion—apply to breaking up a friendship. It's best not to bring a list of grievances, but rather tell the person you're not the best fit for each other and it is time to move on. If you think a public place will steer the conversation and reactions toward the lighter side, meet in a coffee shop. If you expect tears or worse, it might be best to meet privately. This decisive end to a friendship can be painful, but you will be rewarded with a clean and fast break.

You may feel some guilt at letting go of negative people, but you shouldn't. Friendships are supposed to be mutually beneficial relationships. If neither party is benefiting in a positive way, then it is time to move on. To have meaningful relationships you have to be selective about whom and what you give your time to. To be a good friend to five people, you may need to let go of friendships with three other people. You let those friendships go so that those people can move on and give more, and get more, from the friends they have.

Keep Your Inner Circle Small and Exclusive

It's said that we are the sum of the five people we spend the most time with. This is a sobering thought if you have relationships that are on the edge of toxic, or if you have friends that you've outgrown or moved on from. Think carefully about your list of closest confidants and friends. Are they positive people? Do they uplift you? Do you do the same for them? Are they supportive and encouraging, or negative? If you are the sum of the people you spend the most time with, what does that equal?

You can be friendly to anyone, but you can't be friends with everyone. Limit your personal social media connections. If you can truly only remember 150 people, why do you have exponentially more connections than that on social media websites? Why are you reading status updates and looking at photos of people you would never invite over to dinner? It's so tempting to think more is better, when in fact more complicates your life. When you have too many friends to keep up with, you can't build or even maintain your most important relationships.

> **It's so tempting to think more is better, when in fact more complicates your life.**

Cull your personal social media connections. Don't say yes to every request or add every old classmate or coworker. If you feel that you can't remove the connection, then simply block the person's feed. When you're just checking social media once a day (or less) you don't want it clogged with the updates of people you don't see regularly.

Surround yourself with good people in real life and online. If you haven't quite found all those good people yet, be patient. As you find more time for things you enjoy and that give back to you and others, you'll start meeting these people. You may already know some of them but haven't quite made the leap to friendship yet. Be patient and keep your eyes open.

Be Unavailable

Remember when business cards simply had a telephone number and address below a name and title? Today you have three different phone numbers, at least one e-mail address, a Twitter account, Instagram, and maybe even your own website. There are multiple ways to contact you, and you are inundated not only with information but with having to check all these accounts and be available on them.

Turn them off. Disconnect. Make yourself unavailable. Being available and online in seven different places at all hours of the day is the hallmark of the new millennium, and it has made us neither more productive nor happier. In fact, all this availability has only increased our busywork and led to more procrastination and less-meaningful connections. Fight it. Restrict your availability. For personal accounts, decide on an hour of the day, or even a day of the week, to check them and stick to that routine.

While you're at it, reconsider what being unavailable means. When you're unavailable it's because you are doing something so engaging that you don't want to, or need to, stop to update your status or send a photo. When you're unavailable, it means you're truly engaged in what you're doing. You are living life fully. That's worth so much more than responding immediately to a text message.

Let Go of "What If"

It's tempting to use "what if" reasoning to leave your cell phone on and close at hand and to check your e-mail and other online accounts multiple times a day, or even multiple times an hour. What if someone invites me to something? What if there is an emergency? What about that news I am waiting on? "What if" scenarios give us the excuses we need to stay connected and be available all the time.

The problem is that these "what if" scenarios don't leave you time to actually do the work you want to do. You are so busy being available, answering every nonurgent phone call and e-mail and text message, that you can't focus on the important tasks at hand. You can't focus on the things that bring contentment and happiness in the short, medium, and long term. Cleaning the kitchen is interrupted by a query from a friend to meet up or borrow camping gear. You're delayed leaving for work because you got sucked into someone's gossipy status update. A phone call comes in just as you were leaving for a run and answering it steals your motivation to run. Was any phone call, text, or status update critical to you? Did any one require you to drop anything you were doing to help with a true emergency? No.

Rethink what's important information for your life. We so often let our quiet and joyous times be interrupted by the most inconsequential of news. We let that expensive meal out or that Saturday morning sleep-in be stolen or tarnished by our smartphones. Using minimalism to simplify your life can bring many changes and one them is valuing your own time and attention more. Your time is valuable, so be deliberate and thoughtful about what and whom you give it to.

You will be notified of a true emergency even if your cell phone is turned off and you haven't checked in online for twenty-four hours. In a true emergency, someone will come to your house or call your family or friends to contact you—just like in the old days. Our "what if" reasoning is flawed and we use it as an excuse to compulsively be online and available. "What if" is often a crutch for us because we fear that we might be missing out on something.

Fear of Missing Out

All these avenues for interaction and being online anywhere at any time have led to a very real disorder called Fear of Missing Out (FOMO). Someone who suffers from FOMO obsessively checks e-mail and social media accounts because he is worried about not being in the know or missing an invitation. He can't enjoy where he is or the people around him because, through social media, he knows there are other parties or events happening that he is missing. This disorder can be so severe that it leads to depression.

FOMO can also show up in more innocuous forms. Perhaps you see photos online from a friend's vacation and feel bad that you haven't taken a vacation in a while. Sometimes you will even hear that an event or gathering is happening while you're at another social event and regret where you are. You're so fixated on this other activity or event that's happening that you can't enjoy your own activity. The dinner party that you were looking forward to is ruined.

Another side effect of FOMO: you can't commit to social plans far in advance. You deliberate about saying yes or making hard and fast plans for the future because you're worried that a better opportunity might show up. Although cell phones have been fantastic for last-minute gatherings, they have been anathema to last-minute regrets. Do you hide behind a text message and break plans when they end up not suiting your day or because a better invitation comes along?

If you have mild FOMO, if you're often worried that a friend is doing something more exciting than you are or that you've been left off the invite list, try to let go of the constant checking in and updating. Make plans in advance and when you're at an event, turn your phone off. Wean yourself from constant social media check-ins and updates. Put some barriers up if you need to. Ask a friend to hold your cell phone for you. Eventually, leave it at home. Focus on your own plans and aim to be in the moment more. Engage in the places and people around you. You can't fear that you are missing out on something if you are fully enjoying where you're at now.

Minimalist Shopping

Minimalists shop a lot less than other people and with more thought. If you are scared that this life of less means never visiting a mall again, you're wrong. In fact, shopping will be more enjoyable and satisfying than any unplanned shopping spree you've ever had. The secret is very simple: Buy less but buy better.

If you're someone with a closetful of clothes and nothing to wear or a home filled with knickknacks and housewares, none of which bring you joy, your new approach to buying things will feel like a lottery win. Instead of cruising the mall looking for something that speaks to you, something on sale, or an of-the-moment style, you will plan your shopping in advance.

- If you've created a Thirty-Day Buy List, as suggested earlier in the book, you'll know when it is time to hit the mall.

- Before you even step foot in a store you will have narrowed down your purchases to a few makes, models, or colors.

- Because you have planned for this purchase and waited for this purchase and because you now know, after purging your home and closets of a lot of things you never used and spent a lot of money on, that quality is worth the investment, you will finally be able to buy those things that cost a bit more but last a lot longer. There will be no guilt about the purchase because it was planned and budgeted for.

- You won't have to hide anything from your spouse, and you won't have to keep the tags on because it was an impulse buy and you're not sure if it works with anything in your closet.

Quality over Quantity

Much of what we buy today isn't made to last a lifetime. In fact, much of what we buy today is meant to break or wear out long before we're done using it. This is called planned obsolescence. Manufacturers build things to wear out after a set amount of use so that you will buy another newer version of the same product. In some cases, this planned obsolescence is designed to correspond to the changing nature of tastes and fashions, but it is also a built-in way for producers to sell more.

If you've ever been disappointed when a computer stopped working well after a few years or your winter coat only got a few seasons' use before the lining ripped, you are not alone. Most of what we buy now is only meant to last a few years under ordinary wear. By contrast, in the early 1900s, consumer products were meant to last almost a lifetime. Clothing was designed to be altered as styles or the owner's shape changed. Fabric was durable and long-lasting and shoes were reheeled and resoled many times. In the 1920s and 1930s, in an effort to end the Great Depression, manufacturers began building things with shorter life spans to get consumers to buy more and stimulate the economy. Today, planned obsolescence is the norm for most goods, from furniture to work suits.

The solution to these cheap and fast goods is to hunt down quality items that will last longer and can be repaired. Just like when you built your capsule wardrobe, look for classic styles from quality manufacturers:

- Invest in a car from a reputable automaker with a history of vehicle longevity.

- Buy dishes that are timeless in design.

- Get fitted for two excellent bras, one black and one nude, wash them by hand, and get three to five years of use out of them instead of one or two.

Be patient when you do have to buy something and wait until you have found something that will do the job, that you like, and that will last.

Buying fewer things of better quality is a long-term strategy for reducing clutter—and it saves money. Think repair instead of replace and recycle instead of throw away.

Get Over the Desire for More Stuff

We see as many as 5,000 advertisements in a day. Television, newspapers, websites, and billboards are all vying for our attention to sell us something. No wonder we find it hard to resist shopping and wanting more stuff when we get messages to buy things thousands of times a day. And that's just from traditional advertisers. What about our friends and peers showing off a new purchase or modeling a new outfit? There is so much pressure in our lives to buy more things and upgrade every little gadget we own. It's another reason our lives are cluttered with things we don't need or use.

One way to live a simpler and easier life: stop wanting so much stuff. This is no easy feat with all the advertising you see, but there are ways to help you want less without feeling deprived. For example, keep track of when you have an impulse to buy something and try to locate the source of your want. Did you see a magazine ad for a car or did a friend show up with a new pair of running shoes? Are you under some other stress and it's making you pine for a kitchen remodel? Think about the reasons you really want something. Often your wants have little to do with practical needs and everything to do with stress or envy.

To stop wanting more you need to put up some barriers to your triggers. If auto magazines have you frequenting car dealerships and leave you dissatisfied with your own very suitable automobile, stop reading the magazines. If you know that watching a home-makeover show makes you feel unhappy with your living room and envious of the designer interiors, stop watching that television show. You have a choice: You can let those advertisements and triggers make you want more, or you can put on your blinders and continue to enjoy your life with what you have.

Another technique for getting over wanting more is to cherish what you have. That goes for both the physical stuff and the things you can't buy. Treasure your good health, your close friends, the roof overhead, and the food in the refrigerator. When you remember everything you do have it's easier to see that you don't need more stuff cluttering your life.

Enjoying Your Life with Less

After reading all the ways you can use minimalism for a more organized and happier life, you may wonder, what will be left for me to do if I don't have all this clutter and these obligations in my life? It's true, if you don't have all that cleaning to do, all that stuff to pay for, all those extra bills, and all that extra work, you'll have a lot more time and money on your hands. Now:

- You have space in your home.

- You can see the back of your closets and getting dressed in the morning will be a cinch.

- You'll sit down to a home-cooked meal in the evening without any sense of panic about what has to get done before going to bed that night.

- A new sense of calm enters your life and you'll easily be able to decipher true emergencies from inconveniences.

No more piles of things you will deal with later or harried mornings searching for important papers that have been lost in home office clutter. Those things and people you always wished you had more time for? You now have the time. There will be time to sleep in, time for fitness, time to spend an afternoon reading your favorite magazine while soaking in the tub, time to start a new business, or time to just spend more hours on your porch watching the sunset and waving to your neighbors. There is now room in your life for these choices, so enjoy them!

Your
Minimalist
Life

"I am beginning to learn that it is the sweet, simple things of life which are the real ones after all."

—Laura Ingalls Wilder

One thought you might have after minimizing and clearing the clutter: why didn't I do this long ago? The concepts and benefits of living with less are so simple, and you don't need any equipment or special planners to make it happen. Have less and you will have less to do. Just a few hours, some common sense, and a vision of a clear and happy home and schedule can change your life.

As you use the minimalist path to reshape your home and days, remember that you can tailor the degree and areas to which you apply the Do Less concepts however you need them. In certain seasons of your life, a very streamlined home will be your top priority as you go through a particularly busy period with work, activities, or family obligations. At other times, you may want to rein in your social or work commitments for a slower pace of life. The beauty of using minimalism for an organized and happy life is that there is a formula for each person to achieve his or her goals. No one path will be the same as another. The only universal that's true for everyone: we can all enjoy a life of less stuff, obligation, and stress.

About the Author

RACHEL JONAT sharpened her simple-living skills while training and racing internationally as a rower. After multiple cross-country moves, and many trans-Atlantic flights with bags below the weight limit, she retired from the sport after winning a World Championship bronze medal. Rachel used the opportunity of a maternity leave from her post-rowing marketing job to pursue her other childhood dream: writing. She hasn't dressed for the office or attended a Friday department meeting since 2009. Although writing doesn't burn nearly as many calories as rowing, she greatly enjoys all the perks of her nonathlete life, like fewer showers and sipping a cup of coffee while working.

Rachel currently lives in the Isle of Man, a small windswept island in the middle of the Irish Sea, with her husband and two sons. You can read more about her downsizing and minimalist journey at *www.theminimalistmom.com*.